HEALING SOLUTIONS

Goodbye is Not Forever
A Roadmap to Finding Love and Light Again

KENDA SUMMERS

Healing Solutions for Pet Loss

Kenda Summers

Copyright © 2020 Kenda Summers

Cover design by Rob Williams ilovemycover.com

First Printing: December 2020

Kenda Summers is available to speak at your business or conference event. Call (563) 581-9224 for booking information.

ISBN: 978-1-7360585-0-3

WHY READ THIS BOOK
YOU CAN FIND LOVE AND LIGHT AGAIN

When you lose the pet, you love and nothing anyone says or does takes your sorrow away. Do not stop believing – there is a way out of the all-consuming darkness.

With this book I hope to be the person for you that was not available for me when I was lost and fighting to find my way out of the deep sorrow I was in after I lost my Heart Dog Stella.

The answer to moving through grief and finding peace again starts with YOU and understanding what is going on inside of you.

- Grief is the one thing all of us throughout the world will experience
- We can't avoid the pain we feel from loss – but there is support to help you with the sorrow
- We never get over the grief, but we can learn how to become bigger than it

GRIEF HOTLINE INFORMATION

Sometimes you or someone you know needs extra support.

Have you ever said out loud or thought to yourself? - "I am done, I want to be with my pet so bad - I wish I was dead."

This is often referred to as yearning (a feeling of intense longing for something)

If you have felt this way or encountered someone who said this, the conversation that needs to occur next is "Are you thinking of harming yourself".

Often the answer will be "No" of course not – I just miss my pet. Which is perfectly normal, yearning is something that most of us will experience during this grief journey. You wish you were with your pet. There is no intent of self-harm.

The opposite of this is when one has self-harming thoughts. If you have felt this way, or encountered someone else who said this, the conversation that needs to occur next is "Are you thinking of harming yourself." If the answer is "Yes" then a person needs to know that they are not alone, they matter, they are important to this world, but they also need to get some help. A book or FB group is not going to be able to help in this area - a professional counselor needs to be involved. *Suicide hotlines* can provide free and confidential support 24/7.

Important Numbers to know:

National Suicide Prevention Lifeline: 1-800-273-8255

Crisis Text Line: Text HOME to 741-741 (US and Canada)

(UK) Text: 85285

(Ireland) Text: 086 1800 280

Crisis Text Line can also now be reached on FB messenger: https://www.messenger.com/t/crisistextline

DEDICATED TO STELLA, MY HEART DOG.

To one of my best teachers. She left me much too early—and although she is gone physically, she continues to guide me with her wisdom, kindness, and spirit every day as I traverse this grief journey with her spirit supporting me by my side. I will love you and miss you forever my girl.

TABLE OF CONTENTS

Author's Note

It is my hope that this book becomes one of the pieces in the grief puzzle that you are now completing. There are so many pieces that need to be in place in order for you to move through your grief journey, and this book is a wonderful place to start. But it is important to enrich your life with all sorts of healing modalities, and this book will be just one of them. Please note that **this book is not a replacement or substitute for medical or psychological care or grief support.**

Remember, there are many things that you need to immerse yourself in to aid in your healing—things such as journaling, bereavement groups, and professional counselling, if needed. Find people who understand what you are going through. Repeat these words to yourself: "It's okay to not be okay today!" Because one day, I promise, you will find the sunshine again. Let this book be a starting point to your healing. The stories shared in this book come from the broken and healed hearts of numerous pet owners who have faced or are facing the rawness of grief. They share with you their stories of sorrow, happiness, love, and hope that go along with losing something you love so much that can simply never be replaced.

Please join my Pet Loss Facebook Group
at: www.facebook.com/groups/healingsolutionsforpetloss

For more information about my On-Line Grief School please
see: www.petsorrow.com

Acclaim for Healing Solutions for Pet Loss

This book will be an invaluable resource for anyone grieving the loss of a beloved pet. The stories of loss are heart-wrenching, but the strategies for recovery and moving forward are warm and encouraging. Pets are such a big part of our lives, and their time with us is short. It is only when we lose them that we realize how important they are to us. If you have lost a pet or know someone who has, get this book. It will help.

—Sean Michael Andrews, "World's Fastest Hypnotist"

This is a great book for anyone experiencing grief from a loss in their lives, whether it be a pet loss or any other loss. Some things in life, such as grief, just can't be fixed. It exists, and we must acknowledge that fact. Kenda has a loving way to show us that talking through our grief will help us in working through the pain in order to find happiness once again. Through her own experiences, she helps us understand that grief is not something we get over, that it will always be a part of our lives, but that we will be able to move on. She aids us in our journey to reconcile the grief we are feeling by acknowledging our pain and helps us to overcome the obstacles that get in our way. Anyone who has lost a beloved pet will greatly benefit from reading Kenda's new book.

—Mary Carol Trannel, MAC

This is a book for everyone who has ever been through the absolute gut-wrenching loss of a pet. Kenda's experience and strategies will help you in so many ways—both to understand the emotional rollercoaster and to move forward with joy in your heart.

—Sheila Granger, Hypnotherapist

If your loving pet has gone to the Rainbow Bridge, this book will bring you understanding, peace, and comfort. Kenda Summers is the Elisabeth Kübler-Ross of grief for pet loss.

—James M. Vera, Hypnotist and author of *Hypnoketosis*

ACKNOWLEDGEMENTS

There are so many people who have made this book possible.

I thank all of the pets and people who I have loved and lost—I could not have written this book without their wisdom, love, and guidance. Even though so many have left my life, they never left my heart. I work every day with their undying love and support guiding me.

Special thank you to all the contributors who shared a little bit of their heart and soul with all of us. I am grateful for each of you. I am inspired by every story I read. I send each of you much love and support as you continue to heal and grow.

Deep thank you to Stephanie Kiefel Patterson—you will never know how invaluable you were to the success of this book. I was able to trust and do my thing while you worked your magic in editing and making sure everything was perfect. A million thank-you's will never be enough.

And finally, there are two incredibly special people that without their undying support and encouragement I could never have completed this labor of love: Hazel Prosser & Jim Wand. So much love and appreciation to you both.

HEALING SOLUTIONS FOR PET LOSS

INTRODUCTION

My name is Kenda Summers, and I can honestly say that I did not grow up thinking that one day I would be working with grief in the manner that I am.

I mean, do any of us wake up in the morning and think, "When I grow up, I want to be a pet loss grief specialist"? Well, maybe you did, but I know I didn't. I wanted to be an airline stewardess—really! But in Ottawa, bilingualism is a huge deal. While my French is okay, it certainly was not good enough to be considered acceptable to become an airline stewardess—so there went that dream.

But now that I am older, wiser, and more mature, I stop and take a look at where I am in life presently, and I realize that I am exactly where I should be, doing exactly what I want to do—because in this grief arena I can truly be of assistance to those who need help the most: you—the person grieving, the one with the broken heart.

I have so much to say about this, and my hopes are that within the confines of this book I can help you make some sense of what you are going through. I want to share my knowledge, my lessons, my growth, my insight, and my coping skills with you. My hope is that I can help you find you again—the new you. I know that you probably don't like the sound of that. But you are now forever changed—you can never and will never go back to being the person you were. It's impossible.

Maybe your loss happened moments ago. Maybe your loss happened a while ago, but you are still reeling in pain—it does not matter. This book will be right for you no matter where you are on the journey we call grief.

I had an epiphany in 2019 which led me to want to do something, anything, to help people who are grieving. Because sometimes in life bad things happen to good people. Sometimes there is no rhyme or reason why things happen—they just do. They make no sense, and there are no magic words you can say to help people feel better when they are emotionally broken. They need to find their way back to being in control; they need to find their strength. And that can only happen with time.

I wanted to help people find themselves again, so I decided to start a gathering where I could help individuals understand what they were going through. I started a Facebook group that I dedicated to Stella, my Heart Dog. And today that group is thriving and growing every day, filled with incredible, beautiful souls:

https://www.facebook.com/groups/healingsolutionsforpetloss.

The amazing thing about the group is the people who are in it, from the freshly bereaved all the way up to the seasoned healthy griever. With such a diverse group, new people coming in who feel lost and broken get the love and validation they need from those who have gone before them and walked the walk. I believe that when you lose something that you love so much, you need a sandbox to play in where you feel safe, comfortable, and welcome. A place where you can be you.

When I was in school, at recess I always made my way over to the sand boxes to play. There were a few of them, and they were filled with all sorts of kids. I felt most comfortable in the sandbox that wasn't filled with the most popular kids: the one where the nerdy kids and social outcasts were. The kids that didn't quite fit into any group. That is where I found my comfort.

The Facebook group was a great start, but then I realized that I needed to reach more people—so why not write a book to help them get through the difficult times. So that is what I did next. And you are holding the results of that right now. As you work through the book, watch for the (Lesson in Loss) ♡ flags—these mark key concepts that will help you along the way as you heal.

But the Facebook group and the book still didn't seem like enough. I thought to myself that I needed to help people in a more personal way. Since the group is growing more and more every day, I am not always able to stay on top of everything and work with people directly. So I built another Facebook group where I dive deeper into grief, help people understand their feelings, and give them healing modalities to help them deal with stress, anxiety, and sadness. It is so important for your grief to be witnessed, for you to talk about your feelings. When you stuff your feelings down or suffer in silence, that pain comes back around with a vengeance. It will pull you back into its clutches and hurt you even more. Grief needs to be witnessed. For more information about my programs and me, please see my website: https://petsorrow.com

So you are probably sitting there thinking, okay, Kenda what do I do now? I just want to feel better. I just want this pain to go away, I have so many questions, I don't know where to turn. Help me!

Okay, STOP right there! Take a nice, deep breath in through your nose, hold it for a moment, and now release it in a nice, long, drawn-out exhale. I am here for you, and you will be okay. You need support, and supporting people is what I do best.

The first step to walking through your grief starts with you. Telling your story. Finding your sandbox. Understanding your pain, your sorrow, understanding grief.

You need to speak your grief and tell your story. Feel safe, loved, comfortable, and validated. Unfortunately, a lot of us learn about grief based on our upbringing. Did you have an amazing childhood where grief was acknowledged and dealt with in a healthy manner? Great— but if you answered no to this, you are not alone. I for one did not come from a background with a healthy understanding of grief.

We are not taught how to deal with loss. Death is not a subject that we sit around the dinner table and discuss. When you lose someone you love so much, you also lose a part of yourself. The earth keeps spinning, but all you want to do is slow everything down and be still in the moment.

But the bad days need to be lived through—we can't just shut the world off. Well, I guess we can for a little bit—stay home, close the drapes, be alone—but we can do that for only so long. We can be triggered by a sight, a song, a memory, a name, an anniversary, a birthday, a holiday—the list goes on and on. One day you feel fine, and the next you are thrown back into the sadness and despair of what you thought you had worked through.

Within this book I hope you discover and understand that you are not alone. I want you to know that others have felt the pain that you are feeling right now. I want you to look forward to learning more about your feelings and grief in general. I want you to discover the strength inside of you that you may not feel right now. You are stronger than you realize, and you will get through this pain. I will help you—come play in my sandbox and let's heal together.

CHAPTER 1

YOUR WINGS WERE READY, BUT MY HEART WAS NOT

"Information is the resolution of uncertainty."
~ Claude Shannon

Since you are reading this, I send you my deepest condolences, because like me you likely have suffered the loss of your beloved pet. The first time I encountered the quote "Your wings were ready, but my heart was not" (actually the title of a book on grief by Vernessa Blackwell), I couldn't help but align with it fully and completely. It seems that everything that has happened to me my entire life has brought me to this point where you and I meet through my words, and I offer you something that I wish I'd had when I was grieving. You will heal better when you are more educated about what you are experiencing—and that is why I have written this book that you now have in your hands.

Have you ever stopped and looked back at where you are now and wondered, is this it? Is this what I am supposed to be doing, is this where I am supposed to be? I can say I am presently at a point in my life where I am doing what I am meant to do. It feels right; it fits me—just like your favorite sweatshirt and jeans.

I have always been very comfortable with death. If that sounds weird, let me explain. I am not rushing towards death, but I am not running away from it either. I appreciate life and all that it has to offer. I feel very grateful for my health—I have lived a good life. But being around death and loss has helped me understand a world where most people are not comfortable. We are a very grief-illiterate society. I have learnt so much from the people and pets in my life that I have loved and lost. All those lessons, along with the reality and rawness of grief, have shaped me into the person I am today and have made me the perfect individual to help you on your grief journey, which right now likely seems to be engulfing you. But I promise, you will recover and, most importantly, find out more about yourself—more than you ever realized. Life and loss offer us lessons as we travel down that long winding road.

My name is Kenda Summers. I am a Baby Boomer, born into a middle-class family and raised in Ottawa, Ontario, Canada. We led a simple life, where Dad was the breadwinner of the family and Mom stayed home to raise three girls. I have an older sister who is seven years older than me and a younger sister who was three years my junior. I was a decent student at school: never graduated top of my class, but I was never at the bottom of the class either. Except for gym class—I hated gym class.

My first experience with grief was when my grandmother passed away. I was quite young, so I don't have detailed memories of what losing her was like. I just recall her being very sick and weak—and then not being there anymore.

My next experience with grief came when I lost my grandfather. What I recall most from his death was being upstairs in his bedroom, holding a favorite glass of his. I was heartbroken and crying, and I remember throwing the glass down and seeing it break into a million tiny pieces. What happened next stuck with me for a very long time: my mom came running up the stairs and yelled at me for breaking the glass and told me to smarten up and to clean the mess up. I know she wasn't trying to hurt me. I realize now, looking back on it with adult eyes, that she couldn't handle me and the grief of losing her father at the same time. This experience stuck with me, and today when I reflect back on that time, I realize that not everyone will be able to help you when you are grieving, even the ones that love you the most ♡ We need to be okay with that.

The rest of my childhood was pretty uneventful. I grew up, and when I first got married, my husband and I had a hobby farm. I could have as many animals as I wanted! During my childhood, when I made my Christmas list every year, the one thing that I always wanted more than anything in the world was a horse. I was able to finally make that dream come true when we acquired the hobby farm: we bought two horses—and I could not have been happier.

I have always had a passion for large dogs, but my mom and dad were not fans of big dogs. We did have a little poodle named Mitzi, but she was Mom's dog. I think us kids just irritated her. Mitzi tolerated us, but she was definitely a one-person dog, and that one person was my mom. But now that I had my own place, I could have as many dogs and cats as I wanted, in addition to the horses. I was one happy camper!

All was well until my next heartbreaking experience with grief in my 30s: I lost my sister Kimmy and brother-in-law Jeff tragically in a head-on collision with a tractor trailer. This loss was crushing and beyond belief to me. I could not understand how God could allow ething like this to happen to two beautiful people. I am a ristian—but I can honestly say that when I lost Kimmy, I started to se faith in my religion. I was angry, confused, lost, and had no idea how to go on living without her. She was my best friend—just three years my junior, but so wise and so precious to me. She was my everything. And I adored her husband just as much—he was a wonderful man who loved her dearly.

I had started a new job, a position where I knew not a single person. There was no one to lean on and no one to support me. I could not ask for time off as this was a new job, so I did the only thing I knew how to do: to not talk about my sadness or my loss. I stuffed my feelings down and went on about my days like my life was perfect and fine. Boy, was this the wrong thing to do. When we do not deal with grief, when we stuff it down and do not make it a priority—it comes back with a vengeance, and we are so much worse off. ♡ I almost suffered a mental break down many months after the loss—all because I did not have support and wanted everyone around me to believe I was just fine.

It was a long drive home every night, and I would spend most of it sobbing, feeling so brokenhearted and so alone, so very alone. I would have done anything to have my sister and brother-in-law back again. I wanted the nightmare to end. I wanted answers to my questions about why the accident happened. I wanted my old life back. I sought out answers from the police, accident scene re-enactment specialists—anyone who could shed some light on why this had happened. I thought that if I could get my whys answered, surely this seemingly senseless loss would finally make sense.

My sister and brother-in-law had had a dog named Toby that I happily adopted to be my own. He blended in well with my dogs at the time: an English Springer Spaniel named Jake and two Great Danes named Jesse and Brittany. I loved Great Danes, but they are true heartbreakers because they do not live long. When I lost Jesse to an unknown illness, I was completely devastated. I took her to the vet full of hope and prayers but came home alone without my dog.

My husband thought he was doing a wonderful thing by bringing home another Great Dane puppy the very next day. I recall being upstairs when he called to me. As I came down the stairs, I heard the whimpering of a little one. I stopped in my tracks and stared in disbelief—how could he! I was angry, hurt, and stunned—so many emotions were running through my head. I was not ready for this; how could I possibly love this new little one when my heart was broken in two?

But you know what—although my head told me I was not ready to open up again, I took one look at those blue eyes, big floppy ears, and huge feet, and felt my heart start to fill with love again—a different love. I was still heartbroken—but I leaned on this new little one to help me through the tough times.

Eventually I ended up losing my marriage over the loss of my sister. My husband told me that I was too immersed in my grief and that he did not know how to handle me or my emotions. It was just too much for him, so he moved on and found another.

When I look back on it now, I realize how difficult loss can be not only for the griever but for the people around them as well. Through the loss of these two special people I learnt that especially important lesson: a lot of times those who are closest to us are not the ones that will be able to help mend our broken hearts. We need people outside of our circle—people who can relate to exactly what we are going through. ♥

I also learnt that grief does not necessarily have to be the loss of a life. ♥ This is so important for you to realize that I will repeat it a lot. I suffered a great loss when my husband asked me for a divorce.

I had tried everything I could to make things work. We had a child together, Jeffery, who was only 18 months old. But sadly, the marriage was not meant to be, so I had to leave the life, house, and farm that I had grown to love so dearly. And I also had to say goodbye to all my animal friends except for one kitty. I will never forget how I felt as I drove away, looking back in the rearview mirror as my dogs watched me leave, not understanding why they could not come with me. I was so heartbroken, so sad, so lost, so beyond repair—but I needed to be strong for my 18-month-old son. So I became the person I needed to be so that I could raise my son alone and do right by him.

After the loss of my sister and brother-in-law I attended a bereavement session for siblings. I was lost, devastated, and raw with pain—I knew I needed professional help. These group sessions helped me a lot, but after the loss of my marriage I struggled with raw emotions again—so I went to a hospital that offered bereavement group classes. These classes, however, were not helpful because they contained people suffering all different types of losses, which is never a good idea.

Here's what I mean. We went around the circle of participants, each of us telling our stories. After I was done, I immediately felt like I had made a mistake and wanted to run out of there. I was amongst people who had lost very young children, husbands who had lost wives of 50 years of marriage, young adults who had lost mothers or fathers…I am sure it was not on purpose, but I was made to feel that my loss was not as important as all the others—after all, it was just a sister.

I will never forget my ride home—I was a mess as tears streamed down my face. I just wanted Kimmy and Jeff back. I wanted this new reality to not be mine. I just wanted the pain to stop—and most of all I hated that I was made feel that my loss was not significant. All loss is important—all of it!

Looking back, I now know that this incident was one of the turning points that led me to where I am today. I want to inform people around the world that grief is grief and love is love, no matter who that person or animal is. I do not have to tell you—as a pet owner you already know that our pets matter. And so all pet loss matters and is just as important and as gut-wrenching as a human loss. 💔

I decided then and there to take a grief facilitator course so that I could lead my own groups and treat every loss with the respect it deserved. I really enjoyed the class and learnt a lot from it. I went on to volunteer at May Court Hospice in Ottawa. It just felt like something I should be doing: a volunteer job that brought me closer to understanding the depths of sadness, despair, and grief people go through when they lose their everything.

I went on to take another grief facilitator course so I could volunteer at Roger Neilson House in Ottawa, which is a pediatric palliative care facility. That was a tough gig, if I can be perfectly honest—a lot of tears and sadness for all involved.

As time rolled on as it does, I lost my mom, my dad, and a very special uncle. They all have beautiful stories and lessons that I want to share with you, but I will save them for the next book.

I made a lot of changes in the early 2000s: I left a job I had grown to dislike and started a new career in a field that I loved—hypnosis. I entertained people at night as a stage hypnotist and helped people make life changes during the day as a clinical hypnotist. So in 2015 I left behind the Great White North and moved to the Prairie State, otherwise known as Illinois.

It did not take too long to get into the groove of the U.S. I opened my business and found a neat place to hang my shingle in the Land of the Free (Iowa). And it felt good. Everything was aligning perfectly: I was performing stage hypnosis shows at night and doing clinical work during the day. I even managed to perform a stage show in Las Vegas—scratch that from my bucket list.

But my heart was lonely. I longed for a Velcro dog and to hear four little paws on the floor following me around everywhere. It was time to get a dog! But I didn't want just any dog—I wanted a very special dog. A dog I could perform on stage with. A unique well trained, people loving dog—this girl was to be my one in a million. I wanted her to be a pet of course, but I also wanted her to be comfortable in crowds and performing stage. This little dog would become not only my stage sidekick but undoubtedly my best friend forever.

I found a Goldendoodle breeder in Iowa, and my heart fell head over heels in love with the perfect little one. She would be named Stella—Stella the Golden Entrancer. She was such a smart little girl, a real easy keeper. As a pup she appeared on stage with my partner and me at huge national conventions, such as those held by the FFA - Future Farmers of America, where she performed in front of tens of thousands of people. She was a natural and had more than I could have ever imagined or wanted. She was indeed my perfect dog: independent, smart, well behaved, and not afraid or nervous in crowds.

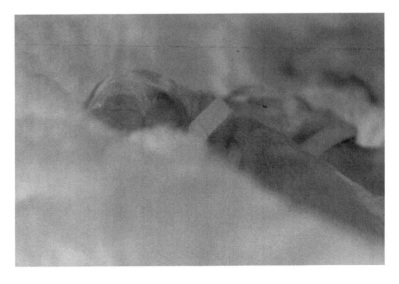

Stella was an easy keeper, she was smart, fun loving, playful, energetic and loved squirrels and rabbits. She spent her free time playing with her two house mates Max and Gabby - Golden Retrievers and evenings performing on stage with me. Life was more than perfect. My heart was truly happy. I got deeply involved in training her with the assistance of a wonderful dog trainer in the area, Robin MacFarlane of That's My Dog. We taught Stella how to retrieve, so my mind was filled with even more amazing ways I could utilize her on stage. I don't think there could be a more perfect dog. Truly.

June 12, 2017, started out like any regular day. Little did I know this would be the day that everything in my life as I knew it would change. It was a warm, beautiful, and sunny day. Stella and I made our way into the office like we did every day. There was a big bay window behind the desk where I worked, and Stella would spend her day there checking for the rabbits and squirrels that dared to trespass on her property.

The office was located on a very quiet street with a posted speed limit of 25 miles an hour, but it seldom saw any traffic. My partner saw Stella whining at the window, so he asked her if she wanted to go outside as he opened the door for her. She almost knocked over her water bowl as she ran from the window to the door all excited. Little did we know what would happen next. He opened the door; she ran off in hot pursuit of a rabbit. We watched in horror as the rabbit ran right across the road just as an 18-wheeler drove by. The rabbit made it, but Stella didn't.

I can still hear myself screaming inside my head every time I re-enact the scene. I knew right away that she did not make it. My partner was beside himself as he ran across the road. One of the tires was on top of her, and he had to ask the driver to back up. He came back across the road with her lifeless body in his arms. I grabbed a blanket and he gently laid her down on it—and that was it. Everything I loved was gone.

So much was running through my head: anger, and then all the questions—why, how, this makes no sense—everything that I am quite sure you felt too. We sat there stunned, not being able to think or move. After about an hour we called our vet and took one last drive with Stella to his office so that we could have her cremated. I did not want to let her lifeless body go. She was my heart dog—how, oh how, could this have happened?! I replayed that final scene over and over and over in my mind. And no matter what, it always ended in the same heartbreaking way. I felt so guilty.

I was a mess, a huge mess. We both were—we had lost our light—and I had the extra stress of forgiveness that I had to find within me. Of course, it was an accident, but we always wonder "what if" and "if only" over and over again, right?

The drive home from the vet's office was the saddest and loneliest drive. Through sobs of pain and grief, I kept looking back into the back seat for my buddy, but she wasn't there—she never would be there again. My heart was cut in half—I was so incredibly heartbroken. I had lost my heart dog—she was never coming back—and I had no idea how I was going to go on without her.

Upon arriving home, Stella's two Golden Retriever playmates, Max and Gabby, escorted our car down into the carport—after all, it was play time, and why did we take so long to get home? There were games to play, sticks to chase, tug of wars to win. I saw their two faces and I couldn't handle it. They came to the door for weeks and weeks looking for Stella. They waited patiently for their Stella to come outside and play with them. They were as sad as we were.

The next day into the office was another hard, hard ride for me, but that was when I received my first sign from Stella: on a large Rubbermaid outdoor storage tub where she would often sit was this huge white feather. I knew it was from her: a message of love telling me that she was okay.

Then when I came home that evening, after I pulled into the carport the late afternoon sky greeted me with the most beautiful rainbow right where she used to play with Max and Gabby. It was almost like she was telling everyone that she was a-okay and had transitioned safely.

That little girl of mine taught me so much about love and loss and healing and living. And I will always hold her in my heart forever and ever.

Fast forward to August 24, 2019, when I heard about a young man who had died in a car accident. I recognized his name and instantly felt sick, wondering if it was the same gentleman I was thinking of. I went to his wife's Facebook page—and sadly, it was indeed him. Reading her post, I discovered that not only he had lost his life, but also the love of their lives, their dog Daisy, had been killed. She was a full sister to my Stella, my heart dog. My heart absolutely ached for all of them.

I attended the husband's wake with our breeder, and, oh my goodness, was it sad. I brought my new Goldendoodle pup Stelly with me because I wanted my friend to know that we also recognized the loss of her four-legged friend. Stelly jumped up on her gingerly and gave her a big kiss—I have tears in my eyes even now as I type this.

After we left the wake, I got an epiphany of sorts on my ride home—suddenly everything that had ever happened to me my entire life, every lesson that I had learnt about grief, everything that I knew and could share, all came together in my mind. I had to do something—that voice inside my head was telling me that this was now my time to put all my education to use to help others who were immobilized due to the pain and numbness of grief.

And the rest is history. I drew on my extensive background as a certified hypnotist, a practitioner of Neuro-Linguistic Programming (NLP), and a grief facilitator to form a loving pet loss support group on Facebook (https://www.facebook.com/groups/healingsolutionsforpetloss).

In addition to giving you the opportunity to connect with others who are grieving the loss of a pet, the group offers a lot of resources to help you better understand the depths of grief. I also created an online grief recovery program for pet loss, available at www.petsorrow.com, where we take a deeper dive into grief. The program will offer mental strategies along with other resources that will help you get through your darkest days and nights so that you can find love and light again.

Now that you know a bit about my journey, in the next two chapters we'll start the complicated task of learning to understand what grief is. And in the remainder of the book, you'll hear from some of the Facebook group members who have courageously shared their stories of loss. When I first conceived the idea for this book, I knew it would have to include those stories, because somehow, we manage, don't we—all of us. We survive the grief, we work through it to the best of our ability, and we always come out learning more about ourselves in the process. I want to share those lessons with you. I want to help you so that you can find your love and light again. Pain from loss is inevitable, but the suffering is indeed optional.

CHAPTER 2

序

WHAT IS GRIEF?

"Grief is like glitter. You can throw a handful of glitter into the air, but when you try to clean it up, you'll never get it all. Even long after the event, you will find glitter tucked into corners. It will always be there—somewhere."

~ Author Unknown

Of all the chapters in this book, this one will no doubt become your most important reference. Think of it as your roadmap to finding love and light again.

When I lost Stella, my heart dog, I did not know where to turn so that I could feel better: a place where I could have all those whys and what ifs answered. So that is what I want to give you: a place where you can have your questions answered. A place where you can understand what you are going through. After all, if we can understand even vaguely what we are going through, it can truly help us to process all those emotions.

I am not sure how you lost your beloved. Your pet might have passed away due to old age or accidently at a young age. Perhaps your pet was sick and needed to be euthanized, or maybe your pet was lost or ran away. Our maybe your pet passed, and you are not sure what happened. The point I want to emphasize is that no matter what the circumstances, all loss counts. One kind of loss may sound more tragic than another, but however it happened, **your loss matters**.

When the word "grief" is mentioned, most people assume that it means the same as "bereavement." But "bereavement" actually refers to *the loss itself*, while "grief" is the *emotional reaction* to the loss. And you don't always have to have suffered a loss to experience the emotional reaction of grief and all its possible impacts on the human body. ♡ We'll see this principle at work when later in this chapter we look at some of the many recognized interpretations of grief.

How Grief Feels

Death is the most recognizable, but certainly not the only, cause of grief—remember how I talked in Chapter 1 about grieving the loss of my marriage? The death can be of a spouse or partner, a parent, a child, any relative who meant much to the bereaved, a friend of many years—or a pet. Grief is the human body's response to the most permanent life-altering circumstance there is: your life has changed forever, and you have to reconcile your feelings to the situation. Grief can be all-consuming and overwhelming. It can be at times sporadic and at others continuous. It can evoke feelings of anger, disbelief, shock, guilt, detachment, fear…the list goes on and on, as each of us is different. Grief can be intense enough to change your eating habits and disrupt your usual sleep pattern; it can cause issues in the workplace and have effects on your physical and mental health.

You may constantly ask yourself questions such as "Why?" or "What did I miss?" or find yourself saying things like "I can't even think straight," "my heart is broken," and so forth. You may feel your world is stationary whilst everyone around you carries on. You will naturally gravitate to those family and friends who you think you can turn to in this most trying time, but you may end up further upset by what you consider to be a lack of empathy, compassion, or interest. Friendships of many years can be lost during this time as you understandably expect more from those around you than they may be able to give.

It could be that the people you're trying to lean on are themselves dealing with the same grief, so they are unable to take yours on board as well. A good example of this is also in Chapter 1: when my mother couldn't handle my grief when we were both mourning the loss of my grandfather. It may also be that those around you, especially those who did not know the departed, simply have no words of comfort to offer, so they resort to clichés such as "At least he/she is no longer suffering," "You made the right decision," "He/she lived to a ripe old age and had a great life"…I'm sure you've heard them all and many more. Or they say nothing because they don't know what to say, leaving you feeling isolated. Whatever kind of responses you get can make you want to withdraw from society so that you don't have to deal with all of this. But I want you to always remember that we are a grief-illiterate society. Even though we have been dying forever, we do not know how to grieve.

The loss of a pet adds yet another dimension to grief, since it seems to the griever that society cares even less about losing a pet than a human. Yet anyone who has lost an animal knows that the grief is just as intense; it just isn't as widely understood by society as a whole. The workplace can be a particular problem: employers can seem very unsympathetic and uneducated about the depths of grieving the loss of a pet. Typically, there isn't any compassionate leave when one loses a pet, so it means the griever using up vacation time (assuming they have some) or taking time off with a doctor's note, even though they're not ill, but grieving.

As we work through the grief, songs, a word spoken in haste—anything—can trigger an emotional response. No one should ever feel embarrassed, guilty, or remorseful when this happens; it's all part and parcel of the grieving process, and each person's grief is unique. During the early days and weeks of grief (the acute phase) you need to be gentle on yourself. Try your best to focus on the good times and try really hard to not allow your mind to take you back to reliving those final moments over and over again. It comes down to the best and most comforting way of dealing with the grief so as to heal yourself.

And cry whenever you need to—don't hold back—let out all those deep-rooted emotions. It is said that one must cry a thousand tears before we begin to move through all the emotions that accompany grief. And it's exactly what the doctor ordered: crying activates the body in a healthy way. When you cry for long periods it releases oxytocin and endorphins—our feel-good chemicals—and these chemicals can help to ease physical and emotional pain.[1]

When I asked members of my Facebook pet loss support group to describe to me what they thought grief was, these are just some of the answers they came up with. In their responses you can see many examples of what we have talked about above:

Pain, longing, emptiness, hollowness, heartache, indescribable sorrow, uncontrollable crying that comes on like waves in the ocean.

The emptiness of waking up, knowing that the love that you shared with the one no longer there will never be there again.

Deep hollow sadness that makes you sick to your stomach and an ache on your heart that will never be repaired.

---

[1] https://www.webmd.com/balance/features/is-crying-good-for-you#1

A heart that has been shattered—only that the pieces are irreparable and hollow when put back together, never to fit back together as they once did.

Grief is the negative emotional state when experiencing a large loss. The stronger the emotional attachment, the greater the pain associated with it, and the longer the duration. It is often associated with and amplified by guilt and shame.

Irreversibility, lack of control, emptiness.

An immense pain and sense of loss that no amount of screaming or crying can even begin to help.

It hurts so badly that it feels unbearable and that your body cannot withstand the emotional and physical pain of the loss.

Pure heartache, total emptiness, tears constantly flowing!

Grief to me varies. When my elderly parents died, I was heartbroken, but was relieved for them that they were no longer suffering and were reunited with their loved ones in heaven. But when my fur babies died, my grief was much more palpable as they were with me 24/7 and needed me as much as I needed them. And the emptiness is much more raw...

Longing for what was...

Love you have to give that has nowhere to go because they're gone.

Grief takes over: sometimes you can't eat, can't sleep, and can't stop crying.

Your heart feels broken. You are lonely and longing for just one more day.

Such sadness that may not be understood by friends and family.

The gut-twisting pain of missing the loved one whom you can no longer see, connect with, or share love with.

Pain—a hole where something is missing and can never be filled.

Missing my girl forever and knowing that the future doesn't include her.

An emptiness, a longing for something I can't ever touch or see or hear. A deep sadness that follows me wherever I go.

All the love I want to give her but never can again.

Dark abyss with a pain that no pill can fix forever.

An emptiness and a desperate longing to see the one you miss so much.

Longing every day to have that beautiful little person back with you physically. And knowing that it is an impossibility until we see them again at the Rainbow Bridge, which feels like hundreds of years away.

Just came back from a beautiful walk in nature. The minute I was at my door, the ache in my heart returned.

It is an emptiness inside, like all that keeps you alive has been torn from you.

How can it be I will never hold, smell, or talk to him/her again?

Gradually the emptiness begins to fill with memories, only to return at times—meaning you have to start over again.

All you know and all you hoped for is gone, and you're staring at a path before you without any understanding of where it will lead.

A lonely journey while the heart is breaking into endless pieces—a journey that no one else can join because they haven't walked in your shoes, haven't shared the same life experiences, haven't got the exact thought processes as you. Hence, grief is a lonely, heartbreaking process which leaves a permanent scar that is invisible to the rest of the world.

When you no longer have a purpose.

A torment and torture to your soul, a feeling of having your heart shattered and your soul ripped from within you—feeling lost and looking for my Bella wherever I go, along roadways, in my backyard and wherever I see woods—knowing that she is gone from the earth but not wanting to accept it. Trying to remember that she is only one heartbeat away just to make it through the day. How else could I go on? I long so very much to be with her that my heart has literally hurt for the past 13 months and 4 days.

To me grief means overwhelming pain in every part of my body and mind. Nothing, even medication, can take it away. There is nothing else like it.

Loss of my soul.

Grief to me is the utter devastation that comes from the anticipation or experience of a loss of a soul who brought love to my life. There are no magic fixes, no time limits, only the acceptance that life is no longer going to be quite the same ever again.

Models of Grief

Now that we know how grief feels, how do we start to make sense of it? A good place to start is with two of my favorite authorities on grief: Elisabeth Kübler-Ross and her associate David Kessler. I follow their philosophy because I can relate to what they have done for those who are grieving. Elisabeth Kübler-Ross was a Swiss-American psychiatrist, a pioneer in near-death studies, and author of an internationally best-selling book *On Death and Dying*, where she first discussed her theory of the five stages of grief, also known as the

"Kübler-Ross model." Although not the only model of grief, it is perhaps the most well-known, dating back to the late 1960s. David Kessler is an author, public speaker, and death and grieving expert. He has published many books of his own, as well as two co-written with Elisabeth Kübler-Ross: *Life Lessons: Two Experts on Death and Dying Teach Us About the Mysteries of Life and Living* and *On Grief & Grieving: Finding the Meaning of Grief Through the <u>Five Stages of Grief</u>.*

> *"We begin to live again, but we cannot do so until we have given grief its time."*

—Elisabeth Kübler-Ross and David Kessler

The "Kübler-Ross model" outlines five stages of grief: denial, anger, bargaining, depression, and acceptance. The important thing to remember, though, is that these stages are not neat and tidy. They are only tools to help us identify what we may be feeling as we learn to live without the one we've lost. ♡ As we've seen many times already, each person's response to grief is unique. And in the same way, the journey each of us takes through the stages is unique. It's also important to realize that the stages do not always neatly follow one after the other in order, nor do they always come one at a time: you might be in one stage for days or weeks, then pass through another very quickly; or you might experience two stages overlapping at the same time, or pivot between two stages very quickly—even within minutes in some cases. Kübler-Ross formulated the stages in order to give us a road map of the terrain of grief so that we can better cope with our losses.

Since Kübler-Ross first formulated the five stages many years ago, there have been many interpretations and variations on them. To find the version which works best for you, I suggest that you google either "the Kübler-Ross model" (it will work even without the dots on the u) or "the five stages of grief" and compare results—there will be a lot of them. You will likely find other models of grief as well, but the basic principles are generally the same. There is a wealth of good information on grief available on the Internet!

Types of Grief

As I mentioned above, there are many different types of grief—over 40, by some counts. Many types overlap and have similar features. Here are some of the most common ones:[2]

Normal Grief

This term is somewhat misleading since, as we've already said repeatedly, there is no typical or average grief. There are no timelines, and grief experiences vary from one individual to another. Normal grief is simply an umbrella term, encompassing all the possible reactions to a loss.

Those reactions can be physical or psychological, and can include (but are not limited to) the following: intense distress, longing, crying, dreaming of your loved one, anger, denial, sadness, despair, insomnia, fatigue, guilt, loss of interest, confusion and disorganization, disbelief, inability to concentrate, preoccupation with thoughts of your loved one, fleeting hallucinatory experiences, meaninglessness, withdrawal, avoidance, over-reacting, numbness, relief, sadness, yearning, fear, shame, loneliness, helplessness, hopelessness, emptiness, loss of appetite, weight gain.

Normal grief is marked by movement towards acceptance of the loss and a gradual alleviation of the symptoms. Those with normal grief generally are still able to engage in basic daily activities.

---

[2] Adapted from https://whatsyourgrief.com/types-of-grief/

Anticipatory Grief

As its name suggests, anticipatory grief is the reaction to a death that you know ahead of time is going to happen. This is one of the types of grief that does not follow a loss. And it's extremely common in cases where your pet has been diagnosed with a terminal illness or has been scheduled to be euthanized. As soon as you accept and understand that your beloved pet is going to die, you begin grieving.

This kind of grief can be confusing: you may feel conflicted or guilty for experiencing grief reactions because your pet is still here. You may experience anger, loss of emotional control, and helplessness.

It's also important to remember that anticipatory grief is different than the grief response felt after a death and does not necessarily make the latter any easier. However, it can allow you to slowly and gradually prepare for and absorb the reality of the loss. And for some people (but certainly not all), it allows you to spend meaningful time with your pet, helping lead to some sense of closure and peace.

Complicated Grief

Complicated grief refers to grief reactions and feelings of loss that are debilitating, long lasting, or impair your ability to engage in daily activities. It's another catchall term, including other types such as chronic grief, delayed grief, and distorted grief (more on those below). The concept of complicated grief, although somewhat controversial, is well known and generally accepted, including by medical authorities such as the Mayo Clinic[3].

Chronic Grief

Chronic grief includes strong grief reactions that do not subside and last over a long period of time, with extreme distress that does not improve.

---

[3] https://www.mayoclinic.org/diseases-conditions/complicated-grief/symptoms-causes/syc-20360374

Delayed Grief

As the name suggests, delayed grief, also known as inhibited grief, is when grief symptoms and reactions aren't experienced until long after a loss or at a much later time than is typical. The griever, who consciously or subconsciously avoids the reality and pain of the loss, suppresses these reactions, usually resulting in physical symptoms. This is why it is so important to allow yourself to fully experience the emotions associated with grief.

Distorted Grief

Extreme, intense, or atypical reactions to a loss, such as odd changes in behavior and self-destructive actions. Anger and hostility towards oneself or others are common.

Cumulative Grief

When one experiences a second loss while still grieving a first loss. This is also referred to as bereavement overload or grief overload.

Prolonged Grief

This is quite similar to chronic grief: grief reactions that are prolonged and intense. The griever is incapacitated by grief, and daily function is impaired on a long-term basis. The griever spends much time contemplating the death, longing for reunion, and is unable to adjust to life without the pet.

Exaggerated Grief

An overwhelming intensification of normal grief reactions that may worsen over time. Characterized by extreme and excessive grief reactions, possibly to include nightmares, self-destructive behaviors, drug abuse, thoughts of suicide, abnormal fears, and the development or emergence of psychiatric disorders.

Masked Grief

Grief reactions that impair normal functioning; however, the individual is unable to recognize that these symptoms and behaviors are related to the loss. Symptoms are often masked as either physical symptoms or other maladaptive behaviors.

Disenfranchised Grief

One's grief is disenfranchised when their culture, society, or support group make them feel their loss or grief is invalidated and insignificant. This can occur when the death is stigmatized (suicide, overdose, HIV/AIDS, drunk driving); the relationship is seen as insignificant (ex-spouse, co-worker, miscarriage, **pet**); the relationship is stigmatized by society (same-sex partner, gang member, partner from an extramarital affair); or the loss is not a death (dementia, traumatic brain injury, mental illness, substance abuse). Obviously, this applies to pet loss—the most common reaction other people have to your loss is likely to be "it was only a pet."

Traumatic Grief

Normal grief responses experienced in combination with traumatic distress suffered as a result of a loved one dying in a way perceived to be frightening, horrifying, unexpected, violent, or traumatic. Distress is extreme enough to impair daily functioning.

Ambiguous Loss

Losses that lack clarity and can lead to different views of who or what has been lost. Individuals and those around them may question whether a loss has occurred or if this is a loss that should validate deep emotional responses, such as with disenfranchised deaths as described above. This could definitely apply to the loss of a pet who has run away.

Abbreviated Grief

As the name suggests, this means a short-lived grief response. The grieving process often seems shorter, and can be due to a number of possible causes such as: the role of the deceased is immediately filled by someone else; there was little attachment to the deceased; or the griever is able to accept and integrate the loss quickly due to anticipatory grief (see above).

I almost hesitated to include this one because it seems so odd— one common explanation for abbreviated grief is "replacement of the deceased such as with a remarriage." This might work in a small number of cases, but as a generalization this just seems ridiculous. Getting remarried—or adopting a new pet—soon after your loss is not necessarily a fast track to end your grief. ♡

Absent Grief

This is when the bereaved shows absolutely no signs of grief and acts as though nothing has happened. It is characterized by complete denial, especially in the face of a sudden loss. This becomes concerning when it goes on for an extended period. But remember— each person's grief is unique, and it's important to note that just because you can't tell someone is grieving, that doesn't mean that they aren't.

I know this is a lot to digest, but please don't feel that you need to completely understand it all at this point. But do refer back to this chapter often as you work your way through the rest of the book. Our next chapter will focus on one of the heaviest emotions to face when working through grief: guilt, which is a major part of the bargaining stage.

Later, as you read the stories from our Facebook group members, see if you can identify some of the characteristics of the stages of grief or the types of grief. The stories of others will hopefully be not quite as painful as your own story, which should make this a little easier. Once you can see what's going on with other people, it will begin to help you understand where you are on your journey and give you a path to follow to finding peace again.

CHAPTER 3

ಯನಿಲ

GRAPPLING WITH GUILT

*"The truth is, unless you let go, unless you forgive yourself,
unless you forgive the situation, unless you realize that the situation
is over, you cannot move forward."*

~ Steve Maraboli

One of the hardest feelings to deal with in bereavement is guilt. I don't think there are very many grieving people I have met who are not riddled with some form of guilt. If you have no guilt or have dealt with it, then please feel free to skip this chapter. And don't feel guilty about doing just that. Not everyone will feel guilt when it comes to their loss. But a lot will, because guilt is very much part of the whole grieving process.

The website dictionary.com defines guilt as the fact of having committed a specified or implied offense or crime. Wikipedia describes guilt as an <u>emotional</u> experience that occurs when a person <u>believes</u> or <u>realizes</u>—accurately **or not**—that they have compromised their own standards of conduct or have violated universal <u>moral</u> standards and bear significant moral responsibility for that violation. Guilt is closely related to the concept of <u>remorse</u> as well as <u>shame</u>.[4]

And to return again to one of my favorite authorities on grief, Elisabeth Kübler-Ross taught that there are only two emotions: love and fear. All positive emotions come from love: happiness, contentment, peace, and joy. Likewise, all negative emotions come from fear: anger, hate, anxiety, and...**guilt**. Love and fear are the only two emotions because they're opposites: we can't feel them both at exactly the same time. If we're in fear, we are not in a place of love. And conversely, when we're in a place of love, we cannot be in a place of fear.[5]

Most grievers will feel guilty in either a tiny way or a huge way, depending on the circumstances surrounding the loss of their beloved pet. You see, we feel guilty when something tragic happens to another. This is because our mind would rather feel guilty than helpless, and so it automatically places us as the one responsible for what happened. We feel that we caused the situation. And the guilt then feeds on itself—it can feel like being on a treadmill that is moving forward so fast you cannot get off, and there is no emergency stop button. That belt just keeps turning and you somehow have to keep moving forward.

How do you feel when I say to you that you are not responsible for what happened? Does it make you feel any less guilt? People will not stop feeling guilty just because you tell them not to feel that way. If I had you read this entire chapter as well as every meme I could

---

[4] https://en.wikipedia.org/wiki/Guilt_(emotion)

[5] https://www.azquotes.com/quote/920213

find on guilt, that would not help you.

In the same way, have you ever tried to make someone feel better when they are feeling bad about something, maybe by telling them that they were not responsible for whatever happened? That didn't work very well, did it? Even though you might believe with all your heart and soul that there is nothing that that person could have done to change the circumstances, you will never change their mind.

Guilt is a feeling, and none of us can talk a person out of a feeling. But please know that just because you feel guilt, that does not make you guilty. I will repeat that sentence—just because you feel guilt, that does not make you guilty. ♡

So, you might be thinking right now, if you cannot take my guilt away, why should I continue to read this chapter? Bear with me—with understanding comes acceptance. And you're absolutely right—I cannot take your guilt away. No one can. What I want is for you to understand guilt, because when you can understand it you will be able to process it, make sense of it, and put it into a healthier perspective as you learn how to cope with your grief. And that is my goal for you. I want you to shift your mind and your thoughts and refocus them with healthier reasoning and healthier internal dialogue. This may seem impossible, but it is not.

Guilt is putting today's knowledge on yesterday's problems.

—T.R. Golden

Let's start with something I know we're all familiar with: negative inner dialogue, which occurs when we want to punish ourselves. Here is a list of common guilt-ridden self-talk phrases that you may recognize:

If only…

I should have…

Why didn't I?

Why did I?

I should not have…

I failed to do this thing…

I did not make the time to….

Why wasn't I…

I wish I would have….

This happened because ……

I honestly believe that when something happens in our lives, we make the best decision we can with the knowledge that we have at that time. It is so easy to look back, immediately have regrets, and start that toxic self-talk: if we knew then what we know now, so many things would be different.

Another really important point I want to make is that when you look back on your situation, what was going on around you at the time? We are influenced by what is happening each moment of our lives. When you think back to what you are feeling guilty about, do you remember those moments exactly as they were? Remember, you can never recreate an exact moment in time. We are always changing—our thoughts, our feelings, the energy around us. And none of us can see into the future or predict what might happen at any one moment—yet we continue to blame ourselves over and over again. It's as if our brains have somehow become lawyers and learned the concept of proximate causation: an event that happened prior to an injury is the direct cause of the injury.

So whatever happened prior to the death—the new food you fed your pet; a the late night at work or an early bedtime that prevented you from being around when disaster struck; you name it—we often will connect it to the death and blame ourselves. And a lot of times these thoughts simply are just not true. We must remember that none of us have the power to stop death. If any of us did, we would be world famous and in great demand everywhere.

Once we realize that no one can stop death, it becomes clear that we must accept the fact that we are not in control. And let's be honest—we control so much when it comes to the lives of our pets: the food they eat, the exercise they receive, the environment they live in, the vet who will look after their health....

Are you the type of person who likes to control things? If so, you may feel more guilt than others because something happened that you could not control. No one likes to admit that they lost control—it is something that you cannot get back.

So this loss of life is truly beyond our comprehension. Our irrational brain will come up with all the things that we should have done, could have done, should have noticed....for if we could have done something different than maybe, just maybe, our pet's outcome would be different. But could it be that in life sometimes things happen that are totally out of our control? When you think about your guilt, is there more to it? Can you look at it and see that it is about control?

Please be careful about allowing your guilt to consume you. Our thoughts are immensely powerful, and they impact us in either a positive or negative manner. And it's not all mental, either—feelings of guilt are carried in our bodies. When you think about your guilt, where do you feel it in your body? Do you feel it in your back, in your heart, behind your eyes? Maybe it feels like a heaviness weighing you down. When people understand guilt better, they often find their bodies also react and release tension, which will allow them to feel much better physically. I like to say the issues are in our tissues, and it is so important to properly deal with the body before something serious happens that affects our health.

But despite the crushing weight of guilt, which can seem like a burden that will never be lifted, there is good news: although things that we couldn't control may have happened, we CAN control our thoughts. Remember that when you change your thoughts, you can change your mind. ♡ Here are two simple but effective techniques to use when you start playing the blame game:

1. Take a moment and loudly say the word "STOP!" Really mean it, really feel it—I want you to startle yourself! And as you say "STOP!" immediately imagine a red stop sign.

2. To combat "I should have..." thoughts, change the thought—reframe it—to "What can I do now?"

It is so important to have your grief validated, to be able to talk things out. Find a friend, a counselor, or a safe, nonjudgmental support group, such as our Healing Solutions for Pet Loss Facebook group (https://www.facebook.com/groups/healingsolutionsforpetloss). Here you will find people who understand exactly what you are going though and a welcoming place to talk about your feelings. I have also created some great educational resources for the group, which can be found in the Popular Topics area on the right side of the page. Here I actually teach people how to shift out of unresourceful states with techniques such as the two described above.

To give you an idea of what the discussions in our group are like, here are some of the responses I got when I asked members about their experiences with guilt over the loss of their pets. How many of these do you connect with?

Guilt. I am dealing with this. Our boy had assistance to die. In my mind I was struggling with a lot of what ifs. He was a big boy—what if we had exercised more? What could I have done differently? The vet had warned us six years ago that big dogs with this surgery lived six to ten years, but the surgery could give out sooner. Then I remember all the good things we did. All the positives. Until that last day he was relatively pain-free: I could not justify him living in pain. I have a voice and I was his advocate. Pet ownership is a responsibility, and we owe them. They trust us. My guilt is lessened, but my grief continues. He has been gone ten days today. I miss him, but I know he is at rest—a well-earned one.

A lot of people feel guilt over euthanasia. My late mother, who was a devout Catholic and had wanted to be a nun, felt tremendous guilt when she had to make the decision to put Mitsie to sleep. Mitsie had cancer.

I knew my Marmalade's quality of life was diminished when he stopped eating and drinking and lost weight. He had lymphoma cancer and now it was my time to give him unconditional love. I had to put his needs before mine in a final act of love, mercy, and compassion. The end was peaceful and dignified: he was with me on a fluffy blanket on my lap. He taught me to let go—that his end was just a beginning, that love never dies, and that love is more powerful than death.

My Chewy died in her sleep at 13 and a half. She was outwardly healthy, happy, and herself. The only thing I noticed after her passing was that she had been on her own just a little bit more, but we have a busy, loud house and maybe she was just in her comfy spots. She still enjoyed her yard, her family, and her routines—she was well to my eyes. I never saw this coming. I never knew she was ill on the inside, and I feel I failed her because I hadn't taken her to the vet for bloodwork or an exam in two and a half years. It never really occurred to me to take the cats because I thought they were well; I *always take someone if I think they're not. My dog went four times this year for minor things and a teeth cleaning, but not the cats. I think Chewy died of heart disease somehow, and at her age it can potentially be tied to underlying diseases such as hyperthyroid or diabetes. I saw and still see no signs she had anything wrong, but I know that cats can hide things, or that symptoms don't always progress the way you would think. Maybe it was only heart disease and she was asymptomatic. From what I have read, the asymptomatic ones respond best to treatment and medication and can live a full life. There's always the chance that the vet wouldn't have heard a murmur or unnatural sounds, but there is also the chance that they could have helped her. I feel like I took her life away by not being a responsible pet owner. We were so incredibly busy and distracted the last two months of her life, and I didn't pay enough attention to her. We didn't have much one-on-one and I can't forgive myself. I loved her so much, and I feel she could be here. She was such a smart, strong, loving girl—she didn't deserve to lose her life. Even if I couldn't have saved her, I wish I could be at peace with the knowledge that I did everything I could and that I had sent her off feeling the best, most special kitty in the world—and I know I didn't. I'm not really coping well, but I also know there's nothing I can do now. I am seeing a grief therapist that specializes in pets. I have a second appointment soon, but I don't really know how I feel about it all yet. All I know is that Chewy trusted me to love and care for her, and I let her down. I MISS HER AND THIS IS SO PAINFUL.*

There are no places or people or even companies that acknowledge pet grief. The loss is as big as losing a spouse or child, and that love is pure, unwavering, and unconditional. Pets love you more than they love themselves. It is okay not to be okay and to cry a river of tears. Only special animal people and special animal grief counsellors understand pet loss. People are uncomfortable about illness, death, grief, and the afterlife, which is part of life.

I have never felt so much guilt as I have since I lost my boy. It consumes me. I know I did everything I could in my power and control—the vets told me. But I still can't help but feel all the guilt.

I still feel guilty about putting Justine, my Galgo (Spanish Greyhound), to sleep. She was losing the strength in her back legs; she collapsed on a walk with me and I had to carry her home. My husband said that she was losing control of her bowels. I booked her into the vet, but on the day she appeared okay and walked okay with me. I took the vet's advice but still don't know if I did the right thing. She passed away in 2014. I also feel guilty that I did not have her ashes and ashes from Juno, another one of my dogs, returned to me.

Still dealing with so much guilt. I just don't know how to put it into words...

Guilt, I wish, if only, all consume me daily. Was it right to let her go? I could see her quality of life was dropping, but did she just need to rest more because she was older? The thing I can't come to terms with is what happened when the vet came to our home. He's been our vet for 30 years, but when he gave her a sedation injection, she screamed. I tried to comfort her but she bit me. Was she telling me she wasn't ready? Who was I to end her life? I know she was suffering and wasn't enjoying life much, in and out of vets, but God, the guilt is huge.

I lost my pup two months ago, but I had no choice: a muscle ruptured in his heart, causing a catastrophic death within ten minutes. And I had just left the vet's office 30 minutes earlier, and he was completely fine. I rushed him back, and he was gone in ten minutes. It killed me to watch and not be able to do anything. The guilt is so bad. And hard to get past. The grief of losing our babies is so real and unbearable. I'm so sorry. This is all too real and hard.

Gosh, yes, the guilt...Guilty for going out for lunch with a friend the day before I had to take him to the vet. If only I'd known, I would never have left his side that day. Guilt for going away camping the weekend before that, not realizing he would be ill as soon as I got back. Now I worry that my leaving him with a friend for four days that weekend caused him so much stress that it made the cancer he was silently fighting catch up with him. Guilt for his last three days on earth, when he was at the vet without me, and I was powerless to change that. Guilt for leaving him for any second for the ten years he was in my life. Guilt for the house moves and relationship breakups and uncertainty and instability I put him through. Guilt for ever taking my eyes off him and for any moment where he was not my number one priority, even though really he always was my number one. My first love and only love, my soul mate, best friend, and reason for breathing. Guilt that he is gone, yet I am still here living without him, when I said that would be impossible. So much guilt and so much pain.

My biggest sorrow that I'm facing right now after the loss of our pet is guilt. His type of cancer was treatable with radiation treatments. It would have been hard on him: four times a week for at least three weeks. He would have had to be sedated completely each time to make sure he didn't move. The main reason we didn't move forward was the expense: it would have depleted our savings. My husband said no, we couldn't do that. I would have spent the money. If I had forced the issue, our pet would still be here.

I could write an entire book on overcoming guilt. I hope you have more enlightenment now when it comes to this emotion, because when you understand guilt, you can overcome it.

Now let's turn to stories from some of our Facebook group members. I won't lie—they will likely be difficult for you to read. But remember to look at them as opportunities to share and understand grief so that we all can heal.

CHAPTER 4

❧

VOICES OF LOSS, HOPE, AND HEALING

"Happiness is beneficial for the body, but it is grief that develops the powers of the mind." ~ Marcel Proust

Now we come to what is in so many ways the heart of this book. You've already heard briefly from some of the members of the Healing Solutions for Pet Loss Facebook group, but now it's time for some of them to tell their stories in more depth. You will very quickly discover one of the main points we've emphasized again and again: everyone's grief journey is unique. I hope that in this wide variety of experiences you can find at least a few that speak to you. And if you're not yet a member of our Facebook group, please consider joining us— our mission is precisely to share these sorts of honest, open, and healing discussions.

In this chapter we'll look at accounts of the early stages of grief. We see raw emotion: shock, emptiness, devastation—these come through in Amy's story about her Bandit. It's not surprising that these are the shortest of the stories, since in the early days of bereavement it is often difficult to find any words at all for what you're feeling. Nevertheless, notice the poem that Cindy wrote for her Zoey, and for the beautiful imagery that Carrley and his wife employ to tell their story from the point of view of their beloved Shebuh.

BANDIT BY AMY

Bandit

I had to put my precious 12-year-old Bandit down suddenly on March 16, 2020. After I noticed red spots on the inside of his legs and his belly on March 13, I called the vet, who said to give him Benadryl and bring him in the next day.

The vet did bloodwork and said that Bandit had a blood disease called immune-mediated thrombocytopenia (IMT). He was put on steroids, but if that didn't work, he would need a blood transfusion. He was pretty much himself over the weekend, other than wanting to eat and drink more often due to the steroids.

My dad took Bandit outside and fed him lunch while I was at work on March 16. He ate and seemed okay. But when I got home, he didn't greet me at the door, which he always did. I had to carry him outside to go to the bathroom; he wouldn't eat his dinner and was lethargic.

I called the vet, who said that Bandit was bleeding internally: he would need an emergency blood transfusion or would have to be put down. I didn't want to put him through the transfusion, which might not have worked. I could tell he was suffering.

I had an hour with Bandit before I had to put him down. I held him in my arms, and his head was on my shoulder when he crossed the Rainbow Bridge. I am beyond devastated. The pain in my heart is unbearable. I live alone, and with everything going on right now, it's awful being at home. Bandit was my heart dog, my child, my entire world.

I cry every day. My life, heart, and home are empty without him.

ZOEY BY CINDY

Zoey

Zoey was my heart and soul, the love of my life, my heart dog. I lost her suddenly on Easter Sunday, April 12, 2020, to pancreatitis, and my life hasn't been the same since. She was only 10 years old. The night before she passed away, I stayed up with her all night because she got so sick so fast. The next morning I took her to the animal hospital. They tried everything they could to save her, but her little body just couldn't fight anymore, and I had to make the heartbreaking decision to let her go. She took her last breath at 5:30 p.m. on Easter Sunday. Just like that, in the blink of an eye, she was gone. It was then that my world went dark.

As I sit here writing, it's been five and a half months since I lost her, and I'm still so devastated. My life has been a nightmare without her. I may be breathing, but I feel like I died with her that day. Trying to adapt and accept my new normal is the hardest thing I've ever had to do. I started talking to a pet loss counselor to help me work through my grief. I also started doing hypnotherapy with Kenda Summers, the author of this book. I've learned that my grief is unique and will take as long as it takes. I need to be gentle with myself.

I honestly don't know if I'll ever get over losing Zoey. Every day is so hard without her. She brought me so much love, joy, and laughter. To have that taken away, especially so suddenly, is too much to bear. I have a cloud of sadness following me around that I can't seem to shake. She was a Yorkie and weighed only four and a half pounds, but her passing has left a huge void. My life is forever changed.

Mommy loves you, Zoey, now and forever. I know you're waiting for me in heaven, and we'll be together again. Until then I'll carry you in my heart.

For Zoey:

Every morning people rise and go about their day.

No one seems to care that you have gone away.

My life is full of emptiness now that we're far apart.

The only place I feel you is deep inside my heart.

I'll never understand why you had to go away,

but I'll try my best to face this world without you day by day.

I'll never forget the day we met and your sweet little face.

The love we shared together can never be replaced.

Now you're up in Heaven waiting there for me.

At least I know you're healthy and happy as can be.

So for now, sweet girl, go play, have fun,

and lie in the sun forevermore.

I'll be content in knowing that when my time comes,

you'll be right there waiting for me at Heaven's door.

SHEBUH'S STORY
BY CARRLEY

Shebuh

One day last week you laid down on the grass as the sun was just coming out. It was warm enough as you rested there like you always do. God came up to you and said hello. He asked if you wanted to walk with him awhile. You answered with "aruff," which was your "sure." As you walked together, you spoke about many things and forgot the time passing by. As you trotted beside him with your little white tail wagging, you walked through fields and flowers, streams and meadows, hills and woods, by oceans and rivers. The wind was blowing in your ears, with both of you laughing and talking. After a while He looked at you and said, "Ya know, we're closer to my home than we are to yours...why don't you just come over and stay with me? Would you like that?" You smiled and said, "Aruff."

He has you now—he's always had you. You were just on loan. I'm selfish, Bubbers—I wanted more time with you. I'm sorry. Forgive me. I can't help it. I know I told you to go whenever you needed to and not to feel bad about it. I have to admit, I lied a wee bit. Forgive me. If it's okay with you, I'm gonna talk to you when I need you. If it's okay with you, I'm just gonna leave a part of my heart I gave to you long ago when you were just a little puppers. You can give it back to me when I see you again, my beautiful white-faced girl.

(Carrley's wife speaks now) I thought about this last night when I was thinking of Shebuh: I imagined God coming to her and asking, "Would you like to go for a walk?" And she said yes, and hobbled along beside Him, and as Carrley said, they were closer to His house than to hers, so He asked her if she wanted to stay with Him. She asked, "What about Mum and Dad?" And God said, "It's okay—they will be sad for a while, and they will miss you, but they will know you are with me and they will be comforted." She then asked, "What about Indi?" And He said, "She will miss you, but I will whisper in her ear that you are with me, and that you are happy and safe. I will tell her that she will have a little sister soon, and that she will need to be a good big sister, like you were for her. I'll also tell her that she needs to support Mum and Dad while they are sad and heartbroken."

Shebuh then asked, "Can I still visit them and watch over them?" And God said, "Of course!" And she said "OK, I'll go home with you," and she then started to walk like a young puppy again. And then they were no longer walking but flying, and her ears were flapping the way she loved, and her lips were flapping. And she arrived at God's house, and there were rooms full of empty peanut butter jars and empty cream containers, and she could miraculously get out every bit—but the fun part is licking them....

CHAPTER 5

cℐ∋

BEGINNING TO COPE

*"Grief can't be shared. Everyone carries it alone; his own
burden in his own way." ~ Anne Morrow Lindbergh*

The shock and emptiness of the first stages of grief can seem like
they will go on forever. However, everyone who has suffered a
loss eventually, at his or her own pace, will begin to process what has
happened and all the emotions that go along with it. As we saw in
Chapters 2 and 3, feelings of guilt and constant thoughts of "if
only..." are extremely common during this phase, and we can see
examples of these in "Indy's Story" by Ani.

All of the authors of the stories in this chapter frankly admit that
they are heartbroken, but notice too how they are starting to come to
terms with their losses by a variety of methods. Jett's mom Lucy
found a compassionate animal communicator, while in a similar way
Nicole welcomed the feelings that her Pacca was still in touch with

her. Cashew's mom Susan started a fund to help pet owners who struggle to pay their vet bills, and Gail plans to volunteer at a shelter in memory of Champagne. And Susi has recognized and treasures the valuable lessons of love and tolerance that her Sky taught her.

INDY'S STORY
BY ANI

Indy

Indy was my constant for twelve and a half years. In every decision I made, Indy was my main and first consideration, and I got so much unconditional love for all the years he was with me. He got me through some hard times in my life, including my divorce. We were inseparable. He was full of life, loving, sweet, a gorgeous cuddle bear. And so smart—I could have a normal conversation with him without any doubt that he understood everything I said.

It never occurred to me that Indy wouldn't be with me one day, until I had to take him to the vet to check on a cough. He had cancer, and the vets couldn't operate. I tried very hard to keep him comfortable for seven months until one day in November 2019 he collapsed. The inoperable tumor had grown so big that it had broken one of his ribs. I couldn't let him suffer—I love him too much for that. I made the decision to put him to sleep on November 26, right before Thanksgiving.

To this day it is very difficult to think about that night. I feared that maybe he thought I betrayed him when I took him to the vet to put him to sleep. Maybe I didn't tell him enough times that night that I loved him. Maybe I didn't kiss him enough. What if I could have kept him through that night and he got better for a few more days or weeks? But then again, what if I had kept him suffering too long? I never again slept in the house where Indy and I lived from the day he left until I sold it. I couldn't stay there without him.

The night Indy was gone, I kept asking him to let me know that he was okay. The next day I saw his face in the sky and a heart right below it. I cried, and it comforted me as I felt it was from Indy. He truly is the love of my life, my soul mate, and I am hoping that I will see him again at the Rainbow Bridge. I am so thankful to Kenda for all her help. I had some very hard nights crying myself to sleep, and her recordings helped me immensely.

I posted the following tribute to Indy on my Facebook page the day after his passing:

My dear Indy boy,

I was so extremely lucky to have shared my life with you for 12 years, 6 months, and 18 days, but it's never enough time. The love that I experienced with you, my Indy, can't be described by any words, but I know that no other love will ever match it.

All the troubles of the world disappeared the moment I saw your face and sat next to you. You always knew how to comfort me and so many of our family and friends. My most amazing memories have been with you. You were the perfect running, hiking, and, later on, walking partner. I loved letting you walk off leash, and you'd listen to me so well when I asked you to go around a muddy spot or untangle yourself from a bush—unless you saw your deer friends, when you would suddenly get temporary hearing loss! And when you'd run away chasing those deer, you'd always find your way back to me, even that time that I was looking for you at midnight with a flash light in the middle of the woods. Finally, two hours later, I saw what I thought was a coyote running towards me. I was so happy to realize that it was you covered in mud. I wanted to smack your butt so bad for giving me a heart attack, but all I could do was hug you like crazy instead when you looked at me.

You, my Indy, were selfless to the very end. Even though you were in such pain and were so uncomfortable sitting down that last day, you waited for all the people that loved you to be there with you during your last moments. Pippi, Oliver, and Mama told me today that they miss you so much.

I wish I could pet and kiss you one more time and sleep in our bed, with you always pushing your butt towards me just to make sure I knew you were right there. I wish I could have taken in all your scent and bottled it up to last me for my whole life. All I have left now is holding your baby dog toy and kissing him like I did you every night before bed. I am finding some comfort in holding your collar and harness, and repeatedly looking at your pictures and videos. I took so many, and I know I annoyed you many times, but you still accommodated me.

The thought of being home without you brings me so much sadness that I can't sleep there anymore. But when I went back for an hour today to grab a few things, I lay down on your red blanket on the couch and sniffed your "old man" sweater that you looked so handsome in.

I am trying to comfort myself by thinking of our beautiful times together. We traveled in many states—not to mention the countless car rides—and you were the best travel companion. I loved it when you wanted to move to the front seat at the most inappropriate times, such as when I was driving 80 mph. But I never denied you. I loved that you wanted to be with me. Hiking a tall mountain, you pooping in the ocean and me asking you in embarrassment to please stop, our recent trip to Chautauqua Lake, you coming to our team's volleyball games and participating as our mascot—these are some of my favorite memories that bring a smile to my face. Oh, and that time you got sprayed by a skunk smack in the middle of your face as you were chasing it. That stink stayed with you for three months, but that never stopped me from giving you kisses.

There is no one like you, my Indy! That special spark in your beautiful eyes never left your face as you aged! They didn't call you Sparky for nothing at the shelter where I found you! (You know that I had to change your name since I found you on Independence Day.) You were so sweet, sharp as a tack, and loving to all dogs and people, especially kids. You put a smile on the face of everyone you met.

I loved it when you were so attentive and participated in people's conversations. I loved that whenever I would get up and leave the room where you were, you'd follow me with your eyes to see where I was going, to judge if I was coming back soon. I loved how at bedtime, if I was still sitting on the couch, you'd abruptly go upstairs and watch me from the balcony, telling me, "Let's go to bed, it's late," and you wouldn't stop staring until I started making my way up to you.

I felt so bad every time I had to leave for work, and you wouldn't want me to go. And many times you would stay right by the laundry room to make your exit into the garage to come with me. Nothing I did could trick you into going back inside the house once you figured out I was leaving. So many times this worked, and I took you with me on car rides, which meant I would have to break the rules and bring you inside stores that didn't allow dogs. But no one said anything when they saw your face. You made people happy, and they couldn't help but stop and pet you. You loved obliging them.

The memories from your last moments are very painful to me. I hope you felt me hovering over you and kissing you everywhere. And I hope you can forgive me if I let you go a day too soon or too late. I did it for you because I saw how uncomfortable you were our last night together. Thank you for sleeping head to head with me during part of that last night—I know you preferred to give me your butt to pet instead.

Please send me a sign that you're now okay, even though you're physically away from me. I have been so worried that you're scared and lonely without me, just like I feel now. Everywhere I go and everything I do reminds me of you. It will be a really hard holiday season not having you next to me, sharing pomegranates, persimmons, chestnuts, and watching a *Twilight Zone* marathon on New Year's Eve. It is so painful not having you here with me. But all this pain is worth it because it means you were such a special, once-in-a-lifetime friend, and I love you more than words can describe. You will always be my number ONE, my Inderz!

JETT
BY LUCY

Jett

How do I go on without you? This is a question I have asked myself a million times. Most of the time, my answer is—all I can do is try.

On July 14, 2020, we celebrated Jett's birthday. Although he had been named that by my daughter, I felt the need to call him "Foof." He was eight years old, my imperfectly perfect sidekick. So excited he was to get gifts. Even though I knew his new toys would be shredded by the day's end, it was worth watching him enjoy.

It was several days after his birthday that Jett refused to eat. I knew something was up as he so enjoyed eating. Jett would help himself to my dinner table without fail—all I had to ask was, "You want to share?" I scheduled a vet visit, and many visits and ultrasounds later, we realized that he didn't have pancreatitis at all. I don't think I will ever forget his last ultrasound visit. The look on the doctor's face told the story: she looked at me and said that evil word—cancer. I think at that moment my heart stopped beating. I squeezed him tightly in my arms and cried like a child. "No, no, you must be mistaken," I said, "he can't leave me, Doctor, he is my best friend." I remember walking down the hall and hearing "I'm so sorry." I think that day a part of me died; half of my heart was cut out.

I asked my daughter May, "How do we know when it's time?" Not just May, but everyone, kept telling me, "You will know." Within days his pain escalated; we had to carry him around. This is not who he was—he was a vibrant, energetic boy who had suddenly gone numb. I asked him many nights, "How will I know, Foof?"

Sunday, several days after his diagnosis, he was in such pain. I stayed up all night into the early morning hours and did my best to keep his pain at bay. That morning he climbed on my leg and placed his head down staring into my eyes. It was then I said to him, "I know I have to let you go, but I can't. How will I go on without you?" At that moment I woke my daughter May and said it was time.

I still do not know how I got the energy to say goodbye. I almost feel like Foof was guiding me through it. I held him close to my heart for the last time on August 11, 2020, as we said our final goodbyes with family around him. "You and me against the world," I whispered in his ear, which was something I always said to him. He was my companion, my confidant, my best friend—he was everything to me. I know it sounds crazy, but to me he was immortal: I never pictured him out of my life. My heart was hollow as I returned home to his bed and toys still in place. I walked around and collected his things and placed them in a keepsake, wiping my eyes along the way. I think I may have asked him to give me strength and guidance.

As I went through the grieving process, I was lucky to have what I call my rock, my daughter May. She held me when I cried and told me that it's okay to cry, as this is how we heal. In my darkest moments I searched the web for support groups to help. I wanted to know that I wasn't alone and that all the emotions that I was feeling were normal. I stumbled on a Facebook group called Healing Solutions for Pet Loss. As I read everyone's stories and cried through all of them, I started to realize that I was not alone. I shared my story, and the outpouring of messages I received was so beautiful. They were all so warm and understanding, and we all shared our thoughts and prayers for each other.

Jett had been every part of my life, so my days were empty and my nights were endless. How could I know that he was okay? I had so many questions. I sought out the help of an animal communicator because I wanted to hear from Jett in his own words—and I found an extraordinary communicator named Melissa. Jett described to her the days leading up to his illness in such detail that I knew he was indeed speaking through her. I asked my questions and he answered. Jett wanted Melissa to relay that he is with me in spirit and that he still sleeps on my pillow every night. I knew that this was his way of letting me know he is with me because I do in fact still put a pillow out for him.

The session with Melissa went on for about an hour. I suddenly felt a warm sense of comfort, the same feeling I would get when Jett was with me. I still look at his pictures and wish I could hold him one last time. I try to remember the enormous amount of love he shared with all of us and that his spirit needed to be free. I will wait until the day we can be together again—I know he will be waiting to walk me through the light.

My beloved, your immortal soul will forever haunt me all the days of my life.

CASHEW
BY SUSAN

Cashew and I bonded from the moment I saw her. I was on my vacation from work, and I said, "If I am meant to get a dog, I will find one this week." And so it happened.

My son had just left home for the U.S. Military Academy at West Point in New York. My husband and I were not allowed any contact with him at all for the first six weeks: no calls, no mail, no nothing. We were devastated to have him gone, and I felt myself sinking into depression. I needed someone to take care of, to fill the void—I missed my son. Once I had Cashew, I knew she was a gift from God.

I had suffered much loss in my life: when I was 16 my mother committed suicide, and my dad died a year later, on my first day of college. Cashew helped me come out of the darkness. Since Cashew was a Jack Russell Terrier, she was small enough to take everywhere. And back then she was not always allowed, but I broke a few rules. We were inseparable.

Cashew had a great life. She went to puppy preschool and doggy day care. One year my husband and I took her along on vacation to Manteo Island, in North Carolina's Outer Banks. At the beach Cashew started to do one of her favorite things—digging—behind where we were lying on our beach towels. We did not know what exactly she was looking for because, being a Jack Russell, she was typically a rodent hunter. So we were just relaxing, but when we looked to check on her, we discovered much to our dismay that she had unearthed a HUGE crab that she was now chasing all over the beach! We were terrified—it was three times the size of our 20-pound Cashew! But she was not the least bit fazed; she just chased it back into the ocean. She was always fierce in hunting mode.

In October 2016 Cashew had a cracked tooth removed, and that was when we found out that she was diabetic. I knew I would do whatever was necessary to help her. I gave her insulin two times a day for a year, and we took her to specialists, but after six months of unsuccessful luck controlling her diabetes, she lost her sight. She became depressed but never left my side.

I promised Cashew I would get her vision back and took her to a veterinary ophthalmologist. But something would always thwart our plans: dry eyes, a corneal abscess—one thing after the other. I put four different drops in her eyes four times a day. The cost of the veterinary bills was mounting. Even though, thankfully, I had pet insurance to help out, I invested thousands—but still I could not help her.

Cashew and I spent a wonderful week together during my vacation the first week of October 2017. But on the morning of October 6 she woke up with an extremely high glucose level and was not herself. I rushed her to the vet, but they sent me home. By lunchtime I knew something was terribly wrong. I was back at vet, who discovered that her stomach was filled with air pressing on her lungs. I had to make the choice to say goodbye to my baby, my best friend of 12 years.

It will be three years next month that Cashew has been gone, and I still cry when I talk about her. But I decided that I had been fortunate to have been able to pay for her medical care because I knew others who would not have been able. So from my loss I started a fund called Cashew's Pawprints to provide those in need with financial help for their sick or injured pets. This has helped me tremendously as I have been grieving. I miss my girl.

PACCA
BY NICOLE

Pacca

In 2004, our second daughter was just a year old and we moved into our newly built house. Since I had had a cat years before, we decided to have one again, and a little tiger cat named Pacca became a member of our family. Because I had little kids, I was always a little cautious—I worried that they would get sick if they played with the cat. So she was outside most of the time. I felt that we did not have a very close relationship—which made me a little sad—but it was okay. Our kids were always trying to eat Pacca's food, so I decided—once again, to keep them from getting sick—that she had to eat outside, in our garage. Sometimes she even slept in the garage, although I felt that she wanted to be with us. The other thing was that I was not happy with was the crazy stuff she did, even though it was normal for a cat: scratching the furniture, using our clothing as a litter box…

When Pacca got older, she was inside with us more often, but still she and I did not have a very close relationship, like she did with the kids and my husband. Her last years were not fun: she began to vomit on a regular basis. And I had to clean up and I was sometimes upset. Finally, I took her to the vet, who told me that she had lung cancer and that there was nothing that could be done. The vet told us that as long as Pacca had no pain and was eating on a regular basis, it was not a problem. That was in 2015. She was often with us, which made us all very happy.

In the summer of 2018 I had the impression that Pacca was not feeling good. She got really calm but had to cough a lot. We knew that it was because of the cancer. She just slept a lot and hung around us. That summer with her was wonderful: when I was lying in the meadow or the grass, she was with me. My impression was that we got closer to one another. Then in the fall she got weaker and started having trouble seeing. We all knew that she would probably not recover. In the meantime, she often slept in our bed and in the house. Everything was there for her.

Several times we thought of going to the vet and having Pacca put to sleep because it was so hard for us to watch her decline, but our impression was that she was still somehow fine. Then she stopped eating, and we knew it was just a matter of days. She got very thin, and so we decided to go one morning to the vet. We were all heartbroken. Pacca was lying on a bed downstairs, and I went to her. I knew that this would be the last time we would have alone. Just us two. In the past I had never had a close relationship with her, although it had grown a little bit over the last few years.

But I never expected what happened then. I felt that I had to put my head next to hers, and I was apologizing for all the years when I had been too cautious with her. The crazy thing was that I felt we were talking to one another in a very intense way I have never experienced in my life. I asked Pacca if she knew what was coming now and explained to her that it hurt us so much, that I loved her so much, and that I was so sorry for everything. I felt she was comforting me, saying that it was okay, that she was not angry at me and understood what was coming. She told me that she was in total peace with that and that I should not worry too much. I was half-sitting, half-lying there at her side, just crying at these words. One part of me said that I was crazy—but this was so real! I have no idea how long I sat there, but it was very comforting for me. Actually, I had wanted to comfort her, explaining to her what was going to happen, but it was the other way around. That was just so amazing—I will never forget those minutes I had with her.

Then my husband and one of our daughters took Pacca to the vet. I could not do it. I wanted to be strong, but I couldn't. Too much pain. Still very touched by what had happened to me, I went into the living room, lit a candle, and played my old dulcimer to express my sadness and pain. I felt the loss, I felt the hole when my husband took her out of our house. Many moments from the past were going through my head. Memories, precious memories. I wanted to be with her at least in my heart and my thoughts as she went to sleep. The loss and the pain were incredible. I never thought I could love this cat so much after not having a very close connection to her from the beginning. But then, while I was playing on my dulcimer with all the loss and grief, something strange happened: all the sudden I had a very strong feeling that she was back in the living room. I could almost feel or touch her. That was so unreal! Even my husband and daughter, when they came home, could feel it. The emptiness, the loss was gone. And it happened over and over again in the following weeks. We could not explain it. But gradually, the visits from Pacca tapered off.

A few months later I was searching the Internet for another cat when I found a little Maine Coon. I had the impression the first few weeks that I still had some contact with Pacca, and I asked her if it was okay to have this new cat. I felt it was totally okay, and from then on, I felt she was gone. Once in a while I can feel her presence, but I know she is happy where she is and that everything is okay. It stills hurts, but we're going to be okay.

CHAMPAGNE, MY BRIGHT LIGHT
BY GAIL

Champagne

Oh, Lordy, where do I begin? My little girl came into my life about three years after losing my other baby girl, Princess, as I just could not bring myself to go through the gut-wrenching heartbreak again. Then one day at work I happened to take a break and look through a local community magazine, where I saw a post about a Miniature Poodle for sale. I immediately called, and the woman said she had two, one male and one female. So I said I would come that night. I called my friend, who said she would come with me. She washed her son's baby blanket and had it all ready when we went at 6 p.m.

When I walked into the room there was one of those domed pet houses, and inside was this little bundle. The woman picked her up (she said the male had been taken), and I reached out to hold this baby girl. The woman said, "She may not go right to you"—the pups were just six and a half weeks old—but I kept my hands held out and she came right into them and put her head right against my heart. That was it—immediate connection, bond, whatever you want to call it. She just snuggled against me and we were one.

I got home, which was all set up for Champagne. I had chosen her name because she looked sparkly, like a glass of champagne. She fit into the palm of my hand and was the cutest. She did cry a little as I set her down to sleep, so I brought her into the bed with me, and off to sleep she went. I even made "addition to the family" announcements with her picture, date of birth, and all that. My daughter told her friends, "I've always wanted a sibling, and look, my mother finally got me one," and showed the announcement. They all laughed.

Since I worked, I had to figure out what to do with Champagne for all those hours. My house wasn't puppy-proofed yet, so I just took her to work with me. Thankfully, my co-worker loved animals too—she had her own fur baby, and we worked in an apartment in mid-town. This was how it continued for quite a while.

Champagne brought a smile to everyone who met her. On the train one day a young girl standing in front of me suddenly cried, "Oh my God, she's real!" and I looked up. Champagne had her head sticking out of the carry case and was looking up at the young girl. We started talking, and the girl said, "This just made my day, as it has been a really bad one." Champagne seemed to be able to sense people's feelings. Another day, I was walking her in front of the house and a sanitation driver literally stopped the truck, got out, and came over to pet and play with her! After about five minutes, the cars behind him started beeping their horns, but he told them to hold on. She just had that effect on people.

This little girl did everything with me: we went to weddings, parties, and holiday events. She was even in a fashion show held by our non-profit, which did lots of events for children. The models jokingly fought over who would get to walk down the runway with her! She loved the ferry going over to Martha's Vineyard Island. The whole town knew her name, not mine. She was such a part of my life, and if people did not see her with me, they would always ask, "Where's Champagne?"

Champagne loved people, other animals, and just enjoying life. She and my friend's kittens would scurry around the living room and play hide and seek, and my friend also let them all on her dining room table to have whatever they wanted. She would watch Champagne for me at times if I had things to do such as a late-night event. If I had not developed such a severe allergy to cats at a late stage in my life, I would have taken on a kitty for Champagne.

I could go on and on with different stories of Champagne and how she brought happiness and joy to all who met her. But she had one little idiosyncrasy: if someone wanted to hold her, she would let them, but only for about five minutes, and then she wanted to come back to my lap or my side. She would let young pups kiss her and play for a few minutes, but then if they got "fresh," she would in her gentle way let them know, and they got her message.

One time on a road trip with my friend Jan and her fur baby

Boomer, we stopped for the night and were all ready to get to bed for our early morning start. Champagne was a few years older than Boomer and sort of the momma. He is a Beagle-hound mix, so you can picture his size next to her. I was in my bed, and Champagne got under the covers to cuddle against my legs, as she often did. Boomer decided he wanted to play and was jumping from his and Jan's bed over to ours. Champagne was tired, and I guess she figured after he had jumped onto our bed a few times, Okay, buddy, that's it. She made those small growling sounds—sort of like when a mom uses her stern voice with her misbehaving children—and got out from under the blankets and face to face with him on top of my bed. Oh, my God, if I had only had a phone that had video feature then! It was too funny. She stood staring at him, and he looked at her like "Okay, Mom," and jumped back onto his bed and stopped. She then gave him one last look and proceeded to go back under the covers. We were hysterical laughing. That was such a fun trip: we drove from New York to Texas, and everywhere we stopped she made friends—with people, children, and other fur babies. To this day it is a fond and funny memory.

There are so many stories I could tell about Champagne's attitude; she had a calming sense about her. She "felt" people and what they were going through, such as with my brother who passed away nine years ago from Amyotrophic Lateral Sclerosis (ALS), also known as Lou Gehrig's Disease. She was with me through all that and with us the minute my brother passed away at home. She would sit and just look at him, and he would look back at her and smile. My brother was nonverbal, but he would nod his head at her and smile. I was sure that she knew what was going on. She was also like this with another person with dementia whom I used to take care of: she seemed to be able to ease the person and relax them. I stopped taking Champagne there, though, as it seemed exhausting for her.

Champagne always gave me strength with her little character. I fell outside on the ice one time at 6 a.m., when no one else was out on the block. She got up on my back as if to protect me…I was in pain, but I was laughing too. I don't know if she thought she could get me up or not. I was on a sheet of black ice, so I managed to shimmy my body to the gate and pull myself up. We made our way home, which was just two houses away, got up the stairs, and spent the rest of the day taking it easy. She always seemed to know when I needed to rest for whatever reason. But most of the time we were two happy campers.

Two and a half years ago I discovered a lump under Champagne's right front leg. The vet said that it was a mass, and during the surgery, they found and removed a couple of other small masses as well. She was 14 at the time, and from then on everything started, one thing after the other. She had another surgery the week after the mass was removed, as they had overlooked something. I could not believe it. My poor baby girl. But she got through it—we both did—and she seemed fine for the most part.

Then one infection after another, one medication after another, sometimes two or three at a time. I changed vets, as I did not have the faith in the ones who had done the surgery. The new vet ran tests, and again more medications. What I called lesions would seem to clear up, then a few months later there were more! The last time I called that vet was when she had another huge lesion. They were not in and told me to come back the next week.

I could not wait, so I then went to my friend's vet and my brother's vet. Mind you, this was exhausting for Champagne—I felt terrible to be putting her through one test after another. It all boiled down to some kind of bacteria. We would think it was cleared up, and then boom, two to four months later, another flare up. There were times she would look at me and I would ask her to please give me a sign. I would cry at times and she would snuggle up to me. She never complained, as I would say; she would just grin and bear it.

The past few months I noticed a change in her: she seemed to forget and would just stand in the middle of the room and stare. She would go to her food or water dish and stare and then walk away. But then she would be fine. The changes in her got more and more frequent. She had always slept with me, but then she started jumping off my bed and would go into the living room. I'm a very light sleeper and would wake up when she did this, finding her on the couch or on one of her beds in the living room. It got to the point where I would let her stay there because when I brought her back into my bed, she would lie for a while and then jump down again and go into the living room. Was this her way of telling me, preparing me that one day she would no longer be there in the bed with me? I think about that now. All the little signs.

She was 16 and a half, and though there were still days when she had her spunk, they were becoming fewer and fewer. She was becoming more anxious around people and did not want to be in a group of more than two or three. She didn't want to go on our normal walks and sometimes didn't even want to go out the front gate—she would turn around and go back to the door to go inside! Her groomer, who used to come to the house, had stopped back in March due to COVID-19, and I totally understood that. I groomed her as best I could, and then a few weeks ago when I was doing her ears, I noticed a bunch of crust. So I cleaned it with her body cloth and applied the ear cleansing that I had from a previous vet visit. A couple of days passed; I checked the ear and again more crust, and the inside was all red!

Jan, my friend with Boomer, was coincidentally taking him to her vet and asked me to go with her. Boomer has a hip problem, so I would often go with Jan to keep her and Boomer company. When we got there, as it turned out, they took Champagne first. She went in with the vet tech, and then the doctor called me—we had to wait outside due to the COVID-19 restrictions. The vet told me that

Champagne had a very bad inner ear infection and described what she wanted to do. I said okay, so she packed the ear because I had told the vet that Champagne would not even let me touch her ear—I did not think I would be able to do everything that needed to be done. Along with the packing was more medication which needed to be administered with food. That was all on a Friday. She had been given a shot of antibiotics and pain medicine, so I would not have to do anything until the next day.

Saturday was okay; I was able to administer the liquid from the syringe into her mouth after she ate. She took the pill easily enough with her peanut butter. But on Sunday it was a bit more difficult, as she did not seem to want to eat at all. I bought some roast beef, roast turkey, cheese, and even a London broil to entice her to eat so that I could give her the medications. (I had always made Champagne's food: homemade chicken, veggies, broth, etc., after recalls so many years ago, and this was what worked best for her.) I made her homemade treats too, and finally got her to take the medication. But she still seemed quite off. I attributed it to her not feeling well and the packing in her ear, which was going to be checked on Friday of the next week. I tried to take her out, but she put on the brakes right outside our door. So, okay, it was back into the house. She seemed to eat less and less. She was drinking water, but it did not seem her usual amount. Yes, people always said I was neurotic when it came to Champagne, but I knew my girl. I knew when things were way off.

On Monday I could not get her to eat anything! I put down three different dishes close to her, as she wouldn't go to her usual food dishes. She would just look, sniff, and turn her head away. I put food in my fingers, and still she would turn her head away. I did finally get the pill into her with peanut butter, but not the syringe full of the antibiotic—I tried all day long, but to no avail.

On Tuesday Champagne was still not the least bit interested in any food, and I finally called the pet hospital again and spoke with the vet tech, as the vet was not in. He told me to closely monitor her: if she vomited, or anything else happened, I should bring her in, but if everything was all good, I should call the next day and speak with the vet.

So I monitored her and everything, but she was the same on Wednesday. I called to explain to the vet all of what was transpiring. The vet said that we could do X-rays, etc., but that I should bring her in. So again, another vet visit that Wednesday. Thank God for my friend Jan, as I knew I could not drive.

At the vet's office, the vet tech came out to get Champagne. Five minutes later the vet called me on my cell phone to report that the infection in her ear was still bad. They were going to repack it and give Champagne a shot of Pepcid as well as an antibiotic shot which would last for two weeks. I said okay.

Back at home, my poor girl just was not herself. I cried and cried. On Thursday, I called the vet as she had directed and told her that there had been no change. I then inquired about euthanasia—I felt her quality of life was at stake and that I had to face the facts. I believe that Champagne was telling me, "Mom, it's time"—she was just giving me the time to be able to follow through.

The vet mentioned X-rays again, but I asked, "To what avail?" I did not want to put my baby girl through any more. I felt it was time. She got the receptionist back to me, and the appointment was set for the next day. And with all this I had totally forgotten that we already HAD an appointment for the next morning—another sign! So, the receptionist said that she'd put the appointment as a maybe, but I said that there would be no maybe about it.

After we got back home, I sat with Champagne. I cried, I talked to her, I petted her, I held her. Then I had to take her out, but once we got outside she did not want to go further. My neighbor's daughter and husband, who were out walking, came over. Champagne let them pet her, but still wanted to go back inside, even when I kept saying, "Let's go see Patrina," another neighbor who spoiled her and whom Champagne loved. I finally picked her up and carried her over to say farewell to Patrina.

We were in Patrina's dining room, and I had to go out to the porch to breathe a bit, so I put Champagne on Patrina's lap. Now mind you, this girl never ever wanted to be on anyone else's lap when I was in her presence. Well, she stayed on Patrina's lap as I walked outside for a minute. I came back inside, and she did NOT go to get off, which is what she would normally would have done. She stayed on Patrina's lap, then I picked her up and we went home.

We—well, I—stayed up most of the night, again holding her on my lap on the recliner. I could not bring myself to go to bed. My friend was going to take us to the vet the next morning, but my brother had called to say he would take me.

So here we are, Friday, October 2, 2020. I called the vet's office to tell them that we were outside. The vet tech came out and took Champagne from my arms. In all this I had totally forgotten to put her harness on, but it worked out fine: I had her in her blanket. The tech told me that the vet would examine her and call me. About 10-15 minutes later the vet called to say the infection was still bad; there had been no change. I told her that Champagne's quality of life was more important to me and that she should proceed. She said okay and did not try to dissuade me, then added that the vet tech would come outside for me so I could be there with Champagne. Thank God she was one of the few vets who, despite COVID-19 restrictions, allowed you to be in the room.

I opened the door, and there was Champagne on the table with a line dangling from her leg. The vet said, "She is ready," and as I walked over to the table my old bubbly girl was there—she was standing on her hind legs, her front legs up against my chest. I picked her up and just held her. She laid her head against my heart as she did so many years ago when I first got her. The vet asked if I wanted to sit with her on my lap, and I said yes. I had her blanket under her and I cradled her in my arms, all the while telling her I loved her, but that she would be seeing so many people who loved her too and that she would feel so much better. And that I would see her again one day. With that the first injection, then the next, and she peacefully went to sleep in my arms. We sat for a few minutes and then I looked up at the doctor with the tears flowing and said, "Thank you."

Things are a bit of a blur after that. I remember walking out to the car, getting home and then just letting the floodgates open. I could not get into my bed that night; I barely slept. The past two and a half weeks have been pure hell. I knew there would be pain and heartache. I knew there would be doubts, but I never thought it would be this bad. I have had fur babies throughout my life and, yes, had to put a couple of them to sleep and felt it, but nothing like this one. My cousin said that it's because she was my "soul pup mate." We could read each other, she understood me, she got me, she made me happy—and I must believe that I made her life as great as I possibly could. I would walk in the door and her face would pop up from the corner of the couch and the tail would wag away. Every morning I would barely get my feet out of the shower and she was licking them. She gave so much joy, like I said, not to just me, but to everyone she came across in life. And yes, I talked to her. People would ask me, "Do you really think she understands you?" and I would say, "But of course, right, Champagne?" and she would wag her tail. People think pets are just animals, but that's not true. I believe they are an extension of ourselves; they are a part of us like no other could ever be.

One night about a week afterwards I was in bed. I finally gave in to sleep, as I had not been getting much at all, and I had a dream. There appeared this beautiful fur baby, in RAINBOW colors, with

Champagne's eyes! Oh my God, I took hold of her and said, "You are so beautiful," and put her up to my chest and kissed her. They were Champagne's eyes! She was telling me that she was okay, that she would always be with me, that all was good. I immediately woke up after this—it was so vivid. You know how you dream in black and white—well, this was full color! Another sign from my girl. I had also seen her in the clouds the day after when I was sitting on my friend's porch, as I had to get out of the house. It was her shape when she would lie down, and my friend saw it too. So I'm not crazy.

So yes, I know it is going to take time. I know the heartache will ease up to a point where the tears will not just flow out every time I think of her. But I must firmly believe that I made the right choice— I had to listen to the signs that she was giving me. My baby girl was tired and decided that she needed to go. I have her ashes, her pictures and videos, some of her toys—but she will always be in my heart until she and I reach out to each other again. Yes, she was my "soul pup mate," and I know there will never be another one like her.

Now I am at an age where I cannot do this again. I can't afford it either, as I'm only on Social Security, but in time I hope to go visit the shelter and sit with those fur babies there. I feel terrible about saying that I can't afford it: I did whatever I could for Champagne, and there was nothing I would deny her. But moving forward, I realistically know that I can't do it. I have had many tell me that I gave her a wonderful life, did all I could, and that, yes, it was time.

Champagne had taught me so much throughout our years together, especially to be more patient and look at things in a different light. She showed me how to be more laid back, as I always would run here, there, everywhere. But right now I am trying to keep myself as busy as possible with cleaning, baking, crocheting, and doing whatever I can to keep myself occupied. We had 16 and a half beautiful years together, and I know we will be together again one day. In the meantime, she is at

Rainbow Bridge romping around, enjoying her forever life.

And in a way writing this has been helpful…although I had to stop a number of times, it felt good to share even if no one else sees it. I will of course print out a copy for myself and keep with my Champagne memory box.

And how ironic that after I wrote all the above, I went outside with a cup of coffee just reflecting on our beginning together, and I had another memory! The house that I live in now was not the first home where Champagne and I started out our lives together. Through the years, we had moved about four times, and my neighbor who had gone with me to get her that first night used to take her on long walks, which we loved. Champagne always took the lead, choosing which direction we went. We passed this house on one of those walks, and I remember commenting how nice it was. Who would have thought those many years ago that this was going to be our last home together!

I'D LIKE TO INTRODUCE YOU TO SKY…
BY SUSI

Skywalker

I was living in a camper van in the south of Spain with my partner and Benjamin, my lovely rescue collie. It was idyllic and a necessary sabbatical from my work in the National Health Service. The sea was but a whiff away, and we nestled under pink pepper trees and eucalyptus. Days were long and lazy, and our walks sublime. We had bought a car because the camper was old and set up with awnings.

I had found a garage that was patient with my "Spanglish," and one day I dropped in to speak to Emilio, as my battery was loose. There were some workmen on the road, and a gorgeous brown puppy was dashing in and out of the forecourt. Emilio ordered a part, and I went back the next day. The puppy was still there. Emilio and I spoke, and it transpired that he was feeding the dog but couldn't take him home, as his "wife would kill" him! I knew of a man up in the mountains who rescued dogs, so I bundled the dog into the car...needless to say, he never went up the mountain.

We called him Skywalker. He was full of worms and completely crazy. He was noisy, causing people to complain about him. He would bite your feet as you walked, and he loved to dig holes everywhere. And he was not fond of other dogs except those in his pack. Yet for all his bluster, he needed gentle handling: he was terrified of sticks, chains, and polo mints. When we took him on an outing to another town, he had a huge panic attack and couldn't walk over a bridge. We avoided bridges after that as he became too heavy to carry. My partner was unhappy and wanted him gone—but I had fallen in love with this nightmare of a dog.

Sky grew to a large black working Labrador cross with Shepherd traits, a stunningly handsome boy, who was high on life, speedy, and completely unaware of his surroundings—causing several visits to Accident and Emergency for me and guests alike. I loved him, and he loved everyone too—often knocking them over in the process.

When Sky was around 17 months old, I was single again and the sabbatical was over. I returned to the UK to secure my life again, whilst he went to a kennel to prepare for his pet passport. He stayed there a year, as he was too aggressive towards the vet who was trying to take blood for the tests. But I could feel him with me, and visitors often commented on seeing a black dog in their peripheral vision. I longed for him to come home.

Finally, his passport was complete, and I prepared to collect him. I had asked the kennel owner not to come to meet me until after I had connected with Sky again. I got out of the car and stood for a moment with tears rolling down my face as I saw my boy playing with another dog scampering around. I waited for them to stop. I spoke his name; he raised his head from the ground, shook it, and then put his head down again. I called his name again; his whole body lifted up and he looked around, shook his head, and looked down again. I shouted his name with a lyrical voice, and he shot up and started running towards me, jumping up the fence and barking like crazy—all witnessed by the kennel owner. He said, "There is no doubt who you are to him."

Our life was wonderful. He was home—my insecure, overenthusiastic dog, aggressive but missing his pack. I bought him a companion puppy, and he was as gentle as a lamb with her, teaching her all he knew—although she never quite understood the digging game.

I employed many dog trainers to support this beautiful, noble boy, but nothing changed—he was a nightmare dog and that was that. I loved him, and he loved me and all my friends who visited. When he was nine he became ill, and we thought we were going to lose him. He had the majority of his pancreas removed, and I had to go to the hospital to feed him, as he was too aggressive with the staff.

He had daily hands-on healing and recovered. He was content, relaxed, and happy, but his fire had died down. We had easier walks but still on a lead if other dogs were around. One day I was channeling

"The Dog Whisperer" Cesar Millan as a rather rambunctious dog headed towards us barking. I pulled Sky close and told the dog to go home in Spanish whilst walking briskly towards the dog. When the dog scampered away, Sky looked up at me as if to say, "You never needed protecting, did you?" He never attempted to protect me again.

Sky was a big dog, and I had always said he wouldn't make old bones—but he lived for five healthy, happy years after his surgery. Eventually, though, he grew weaker and his spirit declined—he was tired. I told him that I would honour his dignity, and whenever he was ready to leave, he had to make it clear to me. One day we went on what I knew would be his final walk—it was too much for him. Content in the garden and trotting around our home, he slept more and more. I cried as I knew the time was coming to say goodbye.

One evening he rose from his bed, trotted over to me, put his head on my lap, raised his eyes to meet mine, closed them, and rested his head again. He repeated this twice, and my heart broke—I knew he was ready.

In truth, my heart is still broken. I loved Sky like no other creature—and I had loved them all. I see him in every black Labrador I pass and especially in my friend's dog Meena—a young black Labrador crossed with a Shepherd—all the joy of Sky without the terrible abuse my boy had suffered.

Sky still visits me; he is still a huge part of my life. He taught me so much about love, tolerance, and enthusiasm for life. He showed me that love conquers all, and no matter what life has thrown at you, you can heal those wounds when wrapped in the arms of love.

CHAPTER 6

❧

ACCEPTANCE AND RESOURCES

"Grief is the price we pay for love." ~ Queen Elizabeth II

As I read through these beautiful stories from our Facebook group members, I was amazed by the resilience and courage of all the writers. Every one of them described fierce battles with overwhelming emotions—yet every one of them keeps on getting up every day and doing the best they can. As we've seen, in the early stages this does not have to be much: just acknowledging your feelings is plenty for a day's work.

The authors of the stories in this chapter have undoubtedly been through very many such days—but they are now starting to reach at least an initial resolution of their grief. It's important to remember that accepting grief does NOT have to mean that you are "okay" with it. You might never be okay with it. You simply acknowledge that the loss has happened and that life has permanently changed.

When I was initially placing these stories into chapters, I was going to make "acceptance" and "resources" two separate chapters. But it quickly became obvious that the two go together: the best way to work towards acceptance of your loss is to find good resources to help you, such as our Healing Solutions for Pet Loss Facebook group (https://www.facebook.com/groups/healingsolutionsforpetloss). The authors in this chapter share a treasure trove of other great resources that can help you find your way back to love and light again. Barbara honors her Scooter's legacy of love and compassion. Maddie's mom Caryn found that journaling has been very helpful for her to work through feeling the pain, which for her was a key part of the healing process. Eva grew to accept the loss of Glader through music, helping other animals, and eventually adopting another Pug of her own. Jim acknowledges that he was fortunate to have understanding co-workers when he was in the early stages of mourning the loss of his Lucky. Lizelle had a disappointing encounter with one counselor soon after losing her QD, but she didn't give up—she persevered and found others who were able to help her. And Lucinda offers great advice, including a surprising suggestion she realized when she lost her Missy: start planning ahead, if possible, to locate resources such as support groups that can help you through those difficult first days after a loss.

Pawsome Pals
By Barbara

Scooter

I've always had a little best friend. Growing up in Brooklyn, New York, my pals were Taffy (a Poodle) and Bambie (a Maltese). My cousin who was a breeder gave my husband and me Bubbles (a Toy Poodle) as a wedding gift—and soon Bubbles was joined by Cookie and Cuddles. The days, which turned into years, were filled with so much love and fun.

A lucky pull of a slot machine led us to Arcadia Pets. It was there that I found my baby boy Scooter, all white and fluffy with big, beautiful black eyes and a smile that made my heart cry with joy. We knew right then and there that he was ours! Upon entering our home, he scooted (ran fast) across the floor, so he became known as our "Scooterboy."

A few months later, my daughter gave us Baci (a Yorkie), and the team of Scooter and Baci was formed, known as Pawsome Pals. For the next 12 years they were inseparable, doing everything together—especially playing together, their favorite pastime. In fact, there wasn't anything they didn't do together!

I do believe they created many imaginary adventures together, such as the time when Scooter and Baci went to meet their friend Sparky at the park. They did their usual running around until Baci's baseball cap flew off from a gust of wind. They all went looking for the cap when they saw that Baci had slipped on leaves and fallen into a hole. Baci was barking as if to cry, "Help me!" and Scooter and Sparky jumped in to save their buddy.

They rubbed their eyes because they could not believe what they saw. It was a mall run by dogs dressed as people! There were all sorts of fun stores: bakeries, toy stores, hot dog stands, rides, and so much more. Although they were having so much fun, Scooter said they had to leave because their moms would be worried. They promised to come back another time!

It's been two years since Scooter left us to go beyond the Rainbow Bridge. We miss his bubbly personality and his amazing wisdom. Scooter had this uncanny ability to sense just the right time to be there for me—I miss that the most. But there's just so much to miss about Scooter: his cheerful bark, his conversations that were so interactive, and his playful energy were just over the top. I truly believe that Scooter was put here on earth to make us happy. And he knew just how to make that happen!

We've had to learn how to continue and move on in the happy world that Scooter created for our family. Baci, who is still with us, is amazing, and I love him to pieces. I know in my heart that these little guys knew how to love and have fun together: that's their legacy to us.

Scooter, who will remain in our hearts forever, taught me and my family about love and compassion. Our puppies are the very best teachers.

Love never dies.

THE STORY OF US
BY CARYN

Maddie

"If there ever comes a day where we can't be together, keep me in your heart, I'll stay there forever."

~ Winnie The Pooh

Sixteen years. Well, if you want to get technical, it was actually 15 years, 11 months, and a week. To some that seems like a blip on the radar, and in all reality, it is a short amount of time, but there was a ton of memories packed into that time. Time is a funny thing, you see—we keep track of seconds, minutes, and hours—but our dogs have no concept of time. They're more present than we humans will ever be.

They say that diamonds are a girl's best friend, but I've never really been about diamonds. All you had to do was look at who was next to me to know that Maddie was my best friend. A confidant, a teacher. But most importantly, a cherished member of the family. I don't know of any being on this planet that knows my every tear and every secret better than Maddie. Before I continue, I think we should start at the beginning of our story.

I had always wanted a dog while growing up. When I was 11 years old, our family finally got one. My sister and I had our mom convinced, but we had to get our dad on board. Finally, he agreed.

During that time, I was in 4-H and knew that I wanted to train Maddie and show her at the county fair. As it turned out, we did so much more: I had no idea that God would give me the passion to train and form a connection with a different species. After some of my mentors noticed my love of training and working with Maddie, the world of competing at local, regional, and national dog show events opened up to me.

Once I learned about dog competitions, I was hooked. While I might someday write a book about our experiences and travels to dog shows, I will always keep those memories locked away deep in my heart. The competitions were a blast, but as I've gotten older, I've realized that the titles, ribbons, and trophies mean so little in the grand scheme of things. They will always be visible, but a special dog will not always be here forever. The miles driven, the hours training, the early mornings at the show, and the laughter with friends are the greatest parts about dog shows.

I often wonder if God knew I needed an earthly companion such as Maddie to get me through those pre-teen years when I was bullied in school. There would be times after school where I would come home and sit and cry with Maddie. She had no judgement—all she had was her love. Sometimes I wonder if He hand-picked her to be in my life for over half of my 27 years thus far, knowing that she would open so many doors for me—that we'd go on so many adventures and meet an abundance of people whom I call my dear friends to this day. It might be crazy to think a dog could do this for one person, but I believe God has done all of this for me. I might have had some basketball dreams that went unfulfilled, but now I can see why those dreams didn't come true: because this was supposed to happen. Maddie was supposed to happen. The people, places, and faces were supposed to happen.

At times I wonder where my life would be today if I hadn't been for Maddie. Would I even have dogs? Would I have gone to the university I went to? Would I work where I work now? What type of hobbies would I have if I had never learned about dog shows? A lot of these questions can't be answered and may never be answered. But one day they will be.

To know Maddie was to love Maddie. I don't think I ever remember a day where she wasn't joyous about life or full of zest to see new people. Maddie was a very social dog and could walk up to anyone, greeting them with a hello and a friendly wag of her tail. She was always fully present in the moment, whether it was basking in the sun in the dining room, lying in the grass in the sun soaking in the rays, or finding a spot of grass or snow to roll in and then lie there afterwards. I firmly believe she came into my life with a purpose to teach me several lessons that I wouldn't have learned elsewhere.

My first two years at college went by in a blur, but I always missed Maddie. To me, she was a constant in my life, even when times were difficult and it felt like the rest of the world had walked out on me. Luckily, my last two years Maddie was able to come to college with me and was the sixth roommate to the girls I lived with during that time. I think she provided comfort for all of them when classes were stressful.

Even at college, Maddie and I went to a local training school every week, which brought more people into our life. This became a very important outlet for me to tune out the stress of school for a bit and focus on something I loved. During the second semester of my junior year, I experienced some health issues of unknown origin for several months, but Maddie was there for me again. She was the reason I got up, got outside, and still trained with her, even if I wasn't feeling good.

After I graduated from college, Maddie and I moved to Green Bay (where she actually had been born) to begin my career. The best part of my new job was that I was able to bring her to work with me, where she received lots of petting and snacks. I think this was the highlight of her day! From here we started a new and different life adventure together. Every transition I faced, we faced it together. Maddie, you were such a trooper, and for that I'm thankful.

And thank you, Maddie, for being the very best teacher a girl could ask for. Thank you for teaching me how to love. Some days I had to put your needs above my own, but it was all out of love. Love is always a choice we make every day—but you, Maddie, never had to choose—you just did. Thank you for teaching me how to be selfless, especially in your older years. Thank you for being that constant in my life and my best friend. No matter how many storms we weathered, we weathered them together. Thank you for your goofy "happy dances," sun bathing, nose nudges, being my hiking buddy, the paw you'd give while someone was petting you, the special quiet moments we shared, and so much more.

Saying goodbye was the hardest thing I ever had to decide for you, and while I wasn't ready, I felt I had to honor you in the best way possible. You had been there for me through everything, and I didn't think it was fair for you to be suffering. I hope you know that my choice was only out of love, and it was the least I could do after all the things you have done for me. While my life will never be the same without you in it, it will be different—a new different. The house certainly isn't the same without you, and it will take me a bit of time to get used to the new normal, but please know I miss you every single day and would give anything to have you back. The hole in my heart will eventually heal, but I know that one day we will see each other again, filled with no pain or sorrow. Please know that I will always love you, and you forever hold a very special place in my heart. You can never be replaced or forgotten. You may be gone from my life, but the memories and the journey we shared were special. Just saying "thank you" doesn't seem like it's enough for your unconditional love, and while I'm only human and made mistakes, you still forgave me. I thank God every day for you, and to Him all the glory!

Life may be different and take some time to adjust to, but I know that Maddie is with me wherever I go. I will always love each and every dog I own, but Maddie will always hold a special place in my heart. She was there through every major life transition: growing up, graduating from high school, spending two years with me and my roommates at college, starting my first real job in a new city, and having my first home. When you look at all of that, it's a lot—way more than most people can ever expect to have with their dogs. For that I am so grateful.

* * *

The above story was written prior to losing Maddie on January 1, 2020. I'm sitting here going on ten months since I've lost her. Reading through some of what I wrote still brings tears to my eyes. I miss her deeply every day. I think writing this out helped me cope with the inevitable. A few weeks after I lost her, I was able to go back and finish what I had started.

There are days where I can't even begin to describe what nine months of grief have looked like for me. There aren't just one or two words that could sum it all up. It has been a roller coaster of emotions. I still have days where the emotions are a bit heavier, and then I have days where things are a bit lighter. I think of Maddie often, and I've even had her visit me in dreams. I still wish she were here today, but I know that she isn't ever coming back.

Maddie was most definitely what I would consider "home": that safe place for me—no matter what was happening in life, she was always there for me. Looking back, I don't think I realized what I had until she was gone. Much of my childhood, my career, my hobby, and a lot of my life revolved around her and what she brought into my life. While my heart may still be shattered, those are the things that I can take with me as I move forward. This is the best way to honor Maddie and the life and memories we shared together.

I wasn't the best at taking care of myself in my early days of grief. Sleeping was hard, eating was difficult, and I couldn't do much of anything else. Probably about two months into the loss, I really started focusing on myself: I made sure that I ate, did some form of movement every day, and did things that filled my cup up. Getting together with friends did help. They often didn't understand the pain I was feeling, but they did provide a distraction from the emotions, even if only for a little bit. I've also found support in places that I didn't expect, and that has helped heal the heart a bit, too. A friend guided me to a pet loss support specialist a few weeks after Maddie had died. The specialist was amazing—I was able to chat with her whenever I needed about the emotions I was experiencing. It was so nice for me to be able to process with someone that wasn't a part of my life but understood the pain I was feeling.

One helpful coping mechanism for me personally was to keep a journal. I didn't have to be a great writer, but I could talk about my day and my feelings. This has also allowed me to look back and realize how far I have come since that point in time when life seemed dark or when I felt like there was no hope. Today I can say that my mentality is much different, even if I'm still heartbroken over the loss. I don't think that will ever change, but I've been able to slowly reconcile with my grief over Maddie and integrate the pain into my life. The gut-wrenching pain certainly has to be felt and acknowledged in order for me to process it and still continue living.

Grief is definitely a very difficult road to walk, often a lonely walk. Now, I don't mean to say that in a pessimistic way. I mean that no one could truly understand my pain because my pain belonged to me. Fortunately, though, there are definitely people out there who have experienced this pain and can companion us on our journey. Thankfully, I was able to find that support, and I cannot tell you how much it has helped me in my own grief experience.

While I could probably write a short story or even an entire book on what I have learned because of my own grief, I will share two insights that have surfaced during this journey.

The first major insight was understanding what grief truly is! Now, that might sound silly, but I had always been under the impression that grief meant sadness and tears. Until I had gone through my own journey, I had no clue what grief really is and what it isn't. Yes, it is sad, and I've shed a river of tears over Maddie. But I didn't know that grief meant so much more: adjusting to a life I didn't ask for, fearing if there was someone else I was going to lose, anxiety about my present life, loneliness, relationships changing, despair, and much, much more. The reality is that grief is not linear. It isn't wrapped up in a nice package with a bow on top—it's actually a really messy process. Sometimes it's waking up at 2 a.m. in tears because I thought of Maddie and how sad I was over losing her. Sometimes it's something else that triggers the tears, such as hearing a song that makes me think of her. There are certainly times where I look at pictures of her and smile, thinking of all the wonderful times we shared together. I think of her when the sun shines brightly, knowing that basking in the sun was one of her favorite things to do. Grief is definitely so many things and is different for each person.

The other thing I've learned is that the grief will last me a lifetime—it will just look different as I travel the journey of life. I have learned that I'm more resilient than I thought I was. Sure, I have been through other hard times, but this has been the single most difficult thing that I have ever walked through in my young life. I would say now that I have more good days than bad—there is hope and light. I can't say that walking this path has been easy, but I can say that I have found peace. It doesn't minimize the loss, nor does it pretend that it never happened, but the days have become a bit easier to bear. While I will never forget Maddie, I know that I can find small ways in the present that will honor her life as I continue to live mine. I believe that one day I will see her again, and that will be the most glorious day.

GLADER
BY EVA

Glader

He had a smile that would make the sun jealous and a personality brighter than the moon and the stars. I was only seven years old when I met Glader, but I'll remember that cold winter day forever. The first time I looked into his eyes I knew that there was nothing I wouldn't do for him. I had dreamt about getting a Pug for as long as I can remember. The house was full of pictures of my parents' Pug, Porter, and these images made me passionate about Pugs for a lifetime. When I first got to hold my very own Pug, I considered myself to be the luckiest person in the world—and I still believe that.

Glader was gorgeous, brave, wild, and playful. He could make me and everyone in our extended family do whatever he wanted, and he always managed to be in the center of things. He could chase my cousin's poodle around the garden for hours, and once or twice he even came close to catching up with our neighbours' cat. He had no problem eating dolls and sofas when he felt that he wasn't getting the attention he deserved, and when our relatives came for a visit he always put on a big show, carrying around their shoes and investigating their purses. One time, when several members of our family were on our way home from a boat trip, he came to meet us a couple of hundred meters from the harbor. My grandparents, who were supposed to be watching him, were really surprised when we returned home accompanied by Glader! He was a rascal through and through, and living with him was an adventure beyond words.

As Glader got older, I would run home from university every day to spend as much time with him as possible. My friends from that period still joke about how I used to buy burgers for Glader on my way home. He also loved buns, and every week we got a plastic bag full of them from my grandmother, who was one of Glader's most loyal servants. Each afternoon, Glader and I ate buns and watched crazy news about Russia's president at the time, Boris Yeltsin. I will always consider those years as some of my favourites.

The day that Glader went over the Rainbow Bridge was the worst day of my life, although I was extremely grateful for his 15 years on this earth. I'm also very thankful that he got to die at my parents' house in my favourite month of the year. It was June 8, and Glader had been really weak and tired for a couple of days. We carried him out into the garden and let him smell his lilac bushes for one last time. We told him how very, very much we loved him, and then we carried him back inside to call the veterinarian—but I never had to place that call. As soon as we laid him down in the bed, he took his final breath.

The years after Glader's death were absolutely horrible. I've never grieved for a human the way I grieved for him, and the healing process was slow, to say the least. I missed his frolics, his smell, his sounds, his smile, his buns, and everything about him and our life together.

Yet I've never felt like I've lost him. I've always known that he's waiting for me on the other side of the Rainbow Bridge, and that he'll be watching over me until then—and that means the world to me.

I also found a lot of strength in my music: I wrote a variety of songs about Glader, and I'm finally planning to release some of them in 2021 or 2022. Another thing that supported my healing process was helping other animals. After Glader's death I became really close to the cats and birds around my apartment and all the animals who visit my parents' garden. I've taken care of limpy jackdaws, disabled crows, hungry sparrows, two old deer, and many other beautiful creatures. Through them I learned how important it is to dare to love again. They have given me more than words can say, and I like to think that I've given them a lot of joy and love in return.

But of course I wanted another Pug as well. I've never wanted children—just pets. Still, it took me 13 years to get a second Pug. Through the years, I looked at many Pugs on the Internet, but I never could bring myself to actually get one. I was so afraid that I wouldn't feel the same love for a new Pug as I felt for Glader.

Then, one magical autumn day in 2012, I saw *him* on a web page—and I just knew that he was the one I had been waiting for ever since Glader left this world. It was something about his eyes that made me feel that I had to make him mine. Then I read the text below the picture and could hardly believe my eyes: his name was Bullen, which in Swedish means "bun"! I just knew that God and Glader had sent this gorgeous Pug to me.

My little bun is lying beside me right now. He's very shy when it comes to strangers, but he rules our home with an iron paw, just like his predecessor did. It turned out that I could love Bullen just as much as I love Glader. Every day with my animals is a precious gift that I can only dream of being worthy of. To me, they are the best proof that love is the greatest healer of all.

Lucky's Story
By Jim

Lucky

One sunny Saturday afternoon back in 2007, I was doing some work in the back garden. Feeling a bit drained from the work, I sat down on the bench with a cold beer. I had just taken a sip and was looking at the back fence when I noticed this black head peeking round the back of the garage from the top of the fence.

There stood this beautiful black cat staring at me, and as I am a pet lover, I couldn't resist calling to him. He jumped into the garden, sauntered over to me, and rubbed himself against my legs. Not wanting to startle him by shouting to my wife, I picked up my phone from the bench and called her to come and see. This gorgeous boy wound himself round both of us in turn, purring like a mini-steam train all the while.

Our resident black mini-panther Gypsy sat at the back door just looking on, not even hissing at him. I still had some work to do in the garden, but the cat didn't seem to want to leave, so I got a garden cushion and laid it on the grass. He promptly lay down on it and curled himself up for a sleep.

When I'd finished, I got him a bowl of water (but no food—he wasn't ours, and he certainly wasn't underfed) and left him to it while I went inside and washed up. When I came back outside later he had gone. Neither my wife nor I thought any more of it.

We didn't see the cat again until about three weeks later. Again he came over the fence and made himself at home on the patio. During these visits all we gave him was water, and each time he came, he just got up and left when he pleased—until one foul, wet day, pouring with rain. He appeared over the fence looking like a drowned rat. I went out, opened the garage, and called him over. He just lay in there for a few hours until the rain died away.

After that the cat came back every day, but each time we refused to feed him. One day my wife decided to put a collar on him, as he didn't have one, and she attached a plastic bag containing our telephone number.

That night we got a call from the cat's owners, and I went round to their place with him. They apologised for any inconvenience, which there hadn't been, and I left it at that—but a few hours later he came back. That particular night was bitterly cold, as winter was setting in.

My wife and I discussed what we should do because neither of us wanted the cat to spend all night out in the freezing cold. I decided to take a sleeping bag into the kitchen and sleep in there with him. He came bolting through the door as soon as it was opened. This time I fed him, as I didn't know how long he'd been wandering outside.

I took the cat back the next day to his owners, who were once again full of apologies. He came back night after night for the next three weeks. Most of these nights were not as cold as that first night had been, so I left him in the garage with a blanket and some water, leaving the garage door up a little so he could get out.

The situation came to a head one Sunday morning. The cat was in the garage sheltering from the pouring rain, looking longingly at the back door. I gave in and let him into the house. After I dried him off and gave him a little food and water, he curled up on an armchair and fell asleep.

A few hours passed and there came a knock on the door. Lucky woke up at the noise and followed me into the hallway. I opened the door to find Lucky's owner standing there drunk. I could smell the alcohol on him, and he was slurring his words. I noticed that Lucky had gone stiff at the sound of his voice, which told me all I needed to know. The owner asked me if I'd seen the cat—I lied and said NO. His reply confirmed what my initial instincts told me: he said not to worry, that the cat had probably run off. And—he wasn't bothered if the cat never came back. It may have been the drink talking, but I doubt it.

I shut the door on him and saw Lucky physically shaking with fear. I picked him up, put him on a chair, and stroked him till he calmed down. While I was talking to the guy, my wife was at the top of the stairs and heard the whole conversation. She agreed we should keep him until she talked to the man's wife, which she did that night.

They no longer wanted the cat, and we were welcome to keep him. We didn't even think twice about it. It was a bit of a struggle with a new cat coming into Gypsy's territory, but after a few months and lots of hissy-spits they got on okay.

Almost three years passed and then tragedy struck. At Lucky's annual checkup his bloodwork revealed that he had chronic renal failure (CRF). For the next three years he was on medication and special diets. Then one November night in 2012, he started walking in circles and meowing like crazy. We rushed him to the vet, who gave him a steroid injection, telling us the next 24 hours would be crucial. Thankfully, he survived those 24 hours.

December came, and so did another attack and yet another steroid injection. This time the vet told us to prepare ourselves for the worst because it might not work. We decided to give Lucky one last chance with the injection, which once again seemed to work.

Then on January 8, 2013, our world came crashing down. My wife called me at work to say that Lucky had had another attack. I rushed home and we went to the vet, who told us that nothing could be done and that it was time to let him go.

The vet said we didn't have to be in the room, but there was no way we were leaving this beautiful boy to see out his final moments in the company of strangers. My wife gently laid a hand on his back and stroked him. As the vet administered the injection, I held his paw. He licked then gently bit my hand as he slipped away.

I have cried over the deaths of humans, but I have never shed so many tears as when Lucky crossed Rainbow Bridge. We decided to have him cremated and his ashes stored in a statue of a sleeping black cat.

For days afterwards I would disappear to the toilet at work and burst into tears, just sitting there until they dissipated. Most of my work colleagues had pets and understood what I was going through, and with the help of my online friends as well I learned to cope with the loss and the grief.

It never goes away, nor will I ever want it to.

Lucky, my bonnie black mini-panther—until we meet again over Rainbow Bridge—

Love,

Daddy

QD
BY LIZELLE

QD

My grief story began on December22, 2017, when I heard the vet say, "I'm sorry—it's bad news." My fur baby, QD, had bladder cancer. It was a few days before Christmas.

QD's favorite thing to do was to open presents, so of course Christmas was always special. Every year we had to give her a gift on each of the few days after Christmas because she would sit under the tree for hours and wait. Her gifts had to be wrapped, and she would open them herself, with a little help. To get that terrible news at that time of year made it so much worse. All the gifts were bought, the celebrations were planned, and I felt like I had to go through everything on autopilot.

Deep down I knew it would be our last Christmas together, but I didn't want QD to see the tears and heartache—I wanted to make it special for her. But she knew me; she could feel I was not okay. Many nights she was the one to lick the tears off my face—she was the strong one. Only later I realised my mistake: I started grieving when she was still with me. I should have made the most of the time we had left. Instead, I fell into a deep depression.

It was such a hard time. The vet kept on telling me we should do chemo, but something just stopped me. I didn't want to put QD through it. She had to be on medication which gave her a bleeding stomach ulcer, and my baby who loved her chicken so much couldn't eat. I kept on falling deeper and deeper into depression. Yet she kept on going, kept on playing, and still loved watching the cats.

As QD got sicker, eventually I just broke down. I'm not a strong person emotionally. I couldn't get out of bed at that stage. I was so depressed. When my mom and sister took her to the vet one morning after a bad night, the vet decided to give her the chemo. QD came back home and ate a whole bowl of chicken. I got hope again: maybe the chemo wasn't such a bad idea. But then the next day she wouldn't eat. When we took her back to the vet, I knew this time I had to go with her. She was put on a drip. That afternoon I was ready to go and get her when I got the call to come: QD was dying. The chemo was just too much for her little body. It was six days before her 12th birthday. Her gift was already wrapped and waiting for her...

Today I still struggle with the fact that I couldn't stay with her till the end. All the light and life had gone out of her eyes; she seemed to look right through me. I gave her so many kisses, thanked her for all the love and incredible years. I told her one more time that I loved her to the moon and back, and then I had to leave: I couldn't let her see me break down in front of her.

That night our neighbors who are pastors came over. Instead of comforting me, the man said that I had to go on with my life; that I had to realize that QD was just gone; that everything we had was over and that I should basically just forget she had ever existed.

But how wrong he was—and QD proved it. She started giving me signs immediately. Actually, the first one came just before I got that terrible call that she was dying: one of her toys, a snowman, fell out of her basket. I picked it up, held it tightly against my face and said, "Baby, in a few hours you will be home." A few days later, after QD was gone, I started seeing snowmen everywhere—so many that I knew it had to be a sign, but I couldn't understand what. One night I spoke to my baby and asked her if she was trying to tell me something. Suddenly it hit me—I remembered what happened that day with the toy. She let me see the snowmen to tell me that she was home: not in the way that I expected—but she was home.

In the same way, every time when I didn't realize at first that QD was sending me a sign, it was like she was giving me a little nudge and saying, "Mommy, open your eyes. I'm right here."

QD was the love of my life. We did everything together. On weekends we would take drives, and she would be the first in the car. Every day we would go for walks, and many days we would spend most of the time in front of my aunt's house, as QD loved to stare at her cats non-stop. She loved watching cats. There was, and still is, such an unbreakable bond between us. She was my baby, my everything. Nothing could or ever would break that bond.

It took me long time to get through the depression. The signs from QD helped me to keep on going, keep on getting up in the morning, but I realised that I also needed counseling and medication. I went to see my own pastor for counseling sessions, and I'm grateful to him. As he is also an animal lover who lost his dog, he understood. I joined amazing groups, and speaking to other people who understood helped so much.

I can always feel QD with me. I won't lie: there are still some difficult days, but that's when she usually shows up with a sign. I try to take a photo of these signs or write them down. I even have a special box where I put all my feathers, flowers, and coins that I get from QD.

Today I'm not on medication anymore and I don't need counseling. I've learned to listen to my heart, to trust the bond I have with my QD. If I had believed my neighbor, if I had believed that she was just gone, I don't know if I would have made it.

This was the most difficult time of my life, but I've grown and learned so many lessons:

I've learned that it's okay to not be okay.

I've learned that it's okay to ask for help.

I've learned to enjoy every moment with the ones I love, to focus on the here and now.

I've learned that some bonds can never be broken.

I know that my baby QD is with me, and I know one day I will see her again. And I've learned that she wants me to be happy: every time I'm sad, her signs are all around me. I just have to open my eyes to see them—or my ears to hear them. One morning I woke up with a song in my head, even though I hadn't heard it in years. It was the first song I received in a sign from her: "I'm Your Angel" by Celine Dion:

And when all hope is gone, I'm here
No matter how far you are, I'm near
It makes no difference who you are
I am your angel
I'm your angel

MISSY
BY LUCINDA

Missy

My dog Missy was not just my pet but my dearest best friend. I used to tell people that she was going to be the maid of honor in my wedding. They would laugh at the crazy dog mom jokes, but I was serious. For the longest time, Missy was my only friend. She was with me when I faced awkward, painful, teenage years. She was with me when I obtained my bachelor's and master's degrees. And until the day she passed away, she was with me as I was working on getting my teaching credential. My Missy never got to have children of her own, but when I was diagnosed with gallstones, she made sure to always be there during the diagnosis and surgical recovery. My Missy lived so long. I know my family and I provided her with the very best life.

But the cancer just kept coming back. She fought so hard during her surgery and rounds of chemotherapy, and she was always brave at the vet's office. The chemo was the worst because we had to wait in the car due to the COVID-19 pandemic.

On June 30, 2020, she was fine. My 15-year-old Lhasa Apso was showing pure signs of strength, jumping and acting like a puppy. But that night, something told me to sleep next to Missy on the floor of our living room. The next morning I woke up to sounds that I had never heard her make—she was struggling to breathe. We rushed her to the vet, who said, "She is telling you that she is done fighting."

To say that my heart broke into a million pieces is an understatement. I held her all the way home. Since the COVID-19 restrictions would allow only three people in the room to say goodbye to Missy, we opted for euthanasia at home. My mom had to make the calls while I just lay next to Missy. I tried my hardest to be strong for her, but I had never felt so broken and weak. I screamed in pain!

The appointment was soon set, and we invited so many people to come pay their respects to Missy. I liked to call them the Missy fan club. When the vet came, he showed us the signs of Missy's overwhelming internal bleeding: her whole underbody was bright red. This cancer was killing her right before our eyes! As the vet injected the medicine, we each got up to tell her goodbye, as the main people in her life were holding and caressing her for the very last time. She sighed deeply and gave us a look of peace and thankfulness.

God gave us a gift that day: when the vet announced that she had passed away, we all noticed that the internal bleeding had stopped. That was God taking away the evil cancer from my precious Missy and letting us know that she wasn't suffering anymore. My dad decided to be the one to carry Missy's body out to the vet's car so that she could be taken to be cremated. He had always loved carrying her, showing her to all her doggy neighbors. July 1, 2020, will always be the hardest day of my life.

If Missy could hear me now through this book, I would just want to say thank you. You were the best part of my life. You taught me how to be kind to myself, and you gave me motherly instincts that I never knew I had. You inspired me to become a teacher! And I know I will see you again, my dear princess. I know we all will. I know you're waiting to watch true crime stories with Mom again. I know you can't wait for Dad so you can help him tend the yard. I know you are waiting to watch sports with your brother. And I know you are sitting with my future kids right now, telling them of all the incredible adventures that you and I shared together. From the food runs, to singing you Elvis songs in the bathroom, to making us matching Halloween costumes—I know these are the stories you are telling them. So thank you, Missy. You will forever hold a big piece of my heart. And as I always say, I LOVE YOU MORE THAN THE STARS! Love, Lucinda

To all of you reading this right now: I know how hard it can be to find resources on pet loss. But they're out there—trust me, I've read every book, have sought counseling, have been to many pet loss support groups, etc. And they all help! You just have to take time do the research, and I would suggest that you do it now, while your pet is still alive. Having a plan is so much better—I wish I had done it.

With the passing of my beloved Missy, I lost so many dear people in my life. So many people who I thought I could count on simply paid their condolences one day and were gone the next. But I made new friendships and bonded with other people. I was very blessed to have a caring family and boyfriend during this experience, but I didn't have the friends—until I started attending my weekly support groups. These people 100 percent get it. They view animals as family, so they aren't going to play down your loss. They care about you and will constantly check on you. In short, I urge you to find a good pet loss support group, whether it be in person or virtual.

I guess I made it a goal early on to take all this pain away in a couple of days—but the loss of a pet doesn't work like that. I've been told that it is going to take years because I had Missy for more than half of my life. I've found that writing letters to my dog has helped tremendously. I am also a musician, so one day instead of writing her a letter, I wrote her lyrics to a song. My dad and I planted a memorial garden for our beloved Missy girl. My mom and I have set up a shelf in our dining room, filled with memories of our Missy. And my brother and I each got customized stuffed animals of our Missy. I don't want to say that these things are magic, but they are making each day a little more bearable.

My counselor told me that Missy left me many gifts, one of which was to be more kind to myself. So that's what I'm telling you: be kind to yourself. Grief from the loss of a pet is real. Do whatever will make you feel an ounce better for the day, even if it's something as small as stepping out your front door for just a minute.

And lastly, I want to say thank you to you. You are reading this book probably because you had a close bond with your pet. It warms my heart to know that I'm not alone—that others also cherish God's creation of animals and love their pets so deeply.

Chapter 7

Pawprints on My Heart

"You cannot prevent the birds of sorrow from flying over your head, but you can prevent them from building nests in your hair."
~ Old Chinese proverb

By Hazel

Oliver, George, & Hugo

Hazel's story spans over three decades and encompasses the loss of not just one but *three* very special cats. Notice how the circumstances of each loss were different—and so were Hazel's reactions. We see so many emotions here: anger, blame (both of which were directed at herself as well as others), guilt, depression—the whole gamut.

Yet Hazel has still managed to come back from each loss and to heal and grow. The most important takeaway from her extraordinary story is simple: not to rush grief simply to please others. The more you try to push grief away, the more it will push back. You need to take time to be gentle with yourself.

* * *

I grew up in a family surrounded by animals. My love for them started at a very young age and has continued throughout my nearly half century of life. I am so blessed to have constantly known unconditional love.

Seeing a little four-legged individual around the home was a given. Not just our pets, either—my mother was a poodle clipper by profession, so it was to be expected we'd see dogs belonging to other families arriving like huge woolly balls and leaving all pristine.

I guess that because of this I knew I'd have animals of my own one day. Once I'd left school and started work, I decided that I really wanted my own cat so that I would have a companion to join me when sooner or later I left home.

The year was 1989. I'd been working full-time for almost 12 months as an estate agent, plus it was the year of my 18th birthday, which I wanted to commemorate. With permission granted by my parents, I started researching suitable, reputable Persian breeders. I loved the Persian's "chocolate box" looks. My employers at the time had Siamese cats; the coat colouration and deep blue eyes really appealed to me, but it was the docile, calm colourpoint Persian my heart was set on.

Conveniently, I located a Persian breeder in my hometown of Sutton Coldfield, England. When speaking to the breeder on the phone, for no specific reason I enquired whether she had any female kittens. The breeder advised me that all the female kittens had been reserved, and her brand-new litter, born on September 2, were all boys. I was invited to see them and ask all pertinent questions about the breed. In those days I hadn't yet learnt to drive, so my boss drove me across town to where I would meet what would become my *own* first cat.

New-born colourpoint kittens are born pure white, their colours starting to show after a few weeks, though the breeder said she had a fair idea of what the colours would be. I gazed at these little white wriggling scraps of fur being nursed by their very proud mama and was smitten. Once I saw the father of these little babies, with his magnificent plush coat, I knew I'd found my new fur-baby.

A couple of weeks later, the breeder called me to confirm the coat colourations of the kittens, one of which was a blue point, as I had hoped. I was once again invited to return and upon doing so named my newly chosen boy Oliver, after the main character in the musical of the same name: he had been feeding but the mother cat moved, so he looked at her as if to say, "Can I have some more....*please*?!" So, my Oliver was there blinking at me through tiny blue eyes.

I had to wait several very long weeks before I could finally bring Oliver home, when he was 13 weeks old. It was just before Christmas, and, being a Persian, he fit right into our family, which included our Tortoiseshell cat Sherry and our dogs: Lady (a Sheltie–Corgi cross), Benji (a Parson Russell Terrier), and Penny (a Toy Poodle). This little boy was so beautiful. I was delighted, in love, and proud as punch.

My parents moved house several times after this, and due to personal circumstances I remained living at home much longer that I would have liked to. Oliver was such a character, and, like his father before him, he grew into a magnificent cat: a proper boy who loved to jump and climb, somewhat unusual for a Persian. He was also unique in that he was very independent, knew his own mind, and liked to go wandering up the garden on his own. But then that's like me, so it worked out well! His blue points deepened, and everyone who saw him usually came out with the same two words: "Oh, wow!"

Upon my return from work each evening, I would spend every moment possible with Oliver, but I could see that he enjoyed being part of a family: he loved Sherry and the dogs. The years flew by, and it was 1996 before I could afford to leave home, due to the economic recession. By that time Oliver was six years old. I secured employment in a completely different part of England—Somerset, to be precise.

Because I was so in tune with Oliver, I wondered how he'd settle away from all he'd known. But I was selfish: he was mine and I wanted him with me! I decided that the fairest thing would be to get him a companion, but judging by the look on his face the day I arrived home with George, I'm not so certain he agreed! That said, other than scowling at George and giving him the odd clip around the ear for being cheeky, Oliver accepted him.

So by November 1996 I was all packed and ready for my new life in an area of the country I was totally unfamiliar with. Oliver, George, and I travelled the 140 miles from the family home to our new rented cottage in Westbury, a small town located in Wiltshire. The cottage was compact and cosy, and there I was, totally confused, with an equally confused Oliver, as well as a 16-week-old kitten, all of us looking at each other as if to say, "Erm, yeah, ok, now what?!" It was dark outside, and I knew absolutely nobody, but I had my two boys with me, so life was to be fresh and new. I felt very grown up knowing that I had to sort myself out for my new job the following day. Only time would tell how happy we would be in our new life.

I have subtly introduced George, but what I failed to say was how his presence would, with the passage of time, literally haul me back from the brink of the deepest grief. But I digress.

George was a lilac colourpointed British Shorthair kitten, born on St. Swithin's Day (July 15) in 1996. As with Oliver, I chose him soon after he was born and named him after my all-time favourite singer, George Michael. Persian coats need an awful lot of maintenance, and whilst I could cope with one, I knew I'd never have the time to establish myself within a new area, settle into a new job, and deal with the coat management of two Persians. So I fell in love with another docile breed, the British Shorthair.

Life in the West Country was really good: my new job, located in the market town of Frome (pronounced "Froom") was brilliant, and despite the deep economic recession at the time, I was enjoying this new independent life. And so was George, whose kitten ways were endearing. Unfortunately, however, Oliver was not happy—in fact, far from it, due primarily to missing his garden.

The house I had rented was a tiny one-bedroom cottage annexe of a very large house, which meant Oliver becoming a true house cat. George was happy with that, but Oliver was not. He had never been totally an indoor cat, so whilst he never ventured away from the back garden, he liked the freedom it gave him. I tried so hard to make Ollie happy. I even took several days off from work to be with him, but when he started to go off his food, I knew something had to be done. With a very heavy heart I drove back up to Staffordshire with two cats in the car, knowing I would only travel back with one. It was so hard leaving Ollie behind with my parents, but he was instantly overjoyed to see the dogs again. I waited and watched him playing in the garden with them before hugging him goodbye with a deep sigh and a heavy heart.

I remember driving back to Westbury with George, feeling overwhelming guilt—yet each time I visited my parents, Oliver was bright and happy, very much enjoying life. But human emotion kept taking over and I found myself thinking things like, Why couldn't you be happy living with George and me, Oliver? Can you not see I love you so very much?! Then I'd see him playing with feathers in my parents' garden or chasing one of the dogs, and my inner voice would say, You've done the right thing, stop it!

For just over a year, George and I shared the cottage. Being so happy living in Wiltshire and working in Somerset, I fully intended to remain there, until one day I answered a surprise telephone call from my former employers, inviting me to return to work for them with the promise of some excellent prospects. Being an ambitious but naïve twenty-something, after spending three weeks procrastinating, I decided to take them up on their offer. So once again life was about to change. It also meant I would need to purchase my own home incredibly quickly: whilst I'd been in the West Country, my parents had moved to a much smaller property, where there simply wasn't room for all the paraphernalia I'd accumulated in the time I'd been away, let alone George and me!

I did find a small house, which was perfect as my first home, plus it had a garden! Oliver visited, courtesy of my mother's transportation, several times. He seemed happy, so Mum said that since he was really my cat, I should try him out to see how he'd settle back with me. Well, he did settle, and I was delighted. I'd got both my boys back with me.

The perfect story never lasts very long, though, does it?

As one often does when buying their first home, I brought in decorators to make the property just right. Oliver's massive moulting coat meant there was loose fur floating everywhere which inconsiderately landed in the paint tins, meaning of course delaying the decorators. They were great with him, but my parents suggested that he spend a few days back with them so that the decorators could finish the job without further delays. I agreed.

Oh, WHY did I ever agree?! This question will haunt me for the rest of my life.

With the decorating finished, house clean and tidy, I phoned my parents with the intention of collecting Oliver. I told my father, who answered the phone, that I was on my way over. I could hear my mother in the background somewhat protesting that it was "too late in the day" and that she'd just got the dogs settled for the night; if I were I to go over now it would disturb them. Mum was always an "early to bed, early to rise" person, but it was only eight o'clock, not overly late by many people's standards.

I wasn't satisfied, knowing that Dad was still very much awake. I was sure that if I went over, he'd have Ollie in his carry case, all ready for me. Unfortunately, my very convincing argument went unheeded. Dad suggested, to save further argument, that I collect Oliver first thing in the morning. I remember that phone call in May 1998 as clearly as if it happened this morning. Reluctantly I conceded and settled down to carry on with a photo collage I'd started.

I so vividly remember picking up a photograph of Oliver that had been taken the previous Christmas, asleep with a big red bow around his neck, purely for the purpose of the photo. I smiled and muttered to myself, "See you tomorrow, Olls". George, who had remained with me whilst the decorators were there since he was a shorthaired cat, looked at me as if I was silly—talking to a photograph! I had literally just picked up a pair of scissors to trim the photo when the phone rang. It was Dad.

A chill went through me as if it were winter. Only it wasn't—it was May, late spring in England. The voice at the other end of the phone was different; it didn't sound like my father at all. I still had the scissors in one hand and was twirling them around my fingers whilst using the other to hold the phone. He said, "It's Oliver…He…" His voice trailed into a muffle. "HE'S WHAT?!" I demanded to know. "WHERE IS HE?!" Dad faltered. Ordinarily if I had spoken to him in such a manner, I'd have been told to change my tone—which confirmed to me that something wasn't right. Dad continued talking in a flat, monotone way, telling me that Oliver had spotted a small open window, and, quite unlike him, had pushed it open further to go outside. "AND!" was my response. It was around ten o'clock and dark outside. That icy chill flew through me once more.

Dad continued, "Hazel, I'm so sorry—he's been hit by a car." Oliver had been sitting under the neighbour's car next door when one of their teenage kids had come home, bent down, and said, "Oh, look at this beautiful cat." Oliver, who was not used to children of any age, shot out from under the car and straight across the road.

The rest, as they say, is obvious. I am not a screamer; I can shout, but not scream—but the noise that emanated would have curdled milk. I slid down my kitchen wall, and the instinctive blame I felt both towards my parents, my mother specifically, but even more so towards myself, was intense. I had never before in my life felt as I did at that moment.

Within a quarter of an hour both my parents were on my doorstep. I refused to let my mother into my home: I thought that all this had happened because she had wanted to go to bed, yet here she was on my doorstep. Dad came in, but Mum's tears from outside my front door were most definitely not welcome. I was in the deepest shock. I don't think I even cried immediately—I'm pretty sure I didn't. I'd heard of this sort of thing happening to other people, but this was me, this was my Oliver. This…was…my…fault!

Dad tried his level best to quieten me, but I think if memory serves me correctly, he pretty much got shown the door too. I sank into my sofa and felt something next to me. It was George, and he stared up at me through his blue eyes, an all-knowing look. I lay on the sofa and stayed there for what must have been 12 hours. George curled up next to me and there he remained, subtly purring in the most genuine, compassionate way. My feline soul mate was there right by my side.

As the days turned into months, I had to wrangle with my emotions: the blame and the bitterness towards my parents, which I guess in hindsight was a little unfair: it wasn't like Ollie had been let outside deliberately. But the "if onlys" wouldn't leave me. It took months to thaw my feelings towards my mother. One day, I heard the song "My Heart Will Go On" by Celine Dion and the words resonated so deeply. To this day, I still can't listen to this song without tears rolling down my face, but the lyrics sum up how I felt towards Oliver:

"Every night in my dreams

I see you, I feel you

This is how I know you go on

"Far across the distance

And spaces between us

You have come to show you go on

"Near, far, wherever you are

I believe that the heart does go on

Once more you open the door

And you're here in my heart

And my heart will go on and on"

Oliver was just eight years old: so young, so much life to live. In my heart eternally.

George and I were inseparable. I clung to him: the fear which engulfed me in the days and weeks following the loss of Oliver was deep. The poor cat only had to sneeze, and I'd have him down at the vet being checked over. The vet ended up telling me I was wasting good money on a perfectly healthy animal, but I was scared. George was fantastic. He never thought of himself as a cat, but he certainly was far too superior to be human. In some ways he was dog-like; in others, he was quite simply George. He was lead trained and car trained; he would sit when asked. And everyone who saw him simply fell in love. George was mine and I was his. If I liked people who came to visit, then so did George—but if anyone else came round, he did a fast disappearing act.

British Shorthairs are large and stocky, and don't fully mature until they are around three to five years of age. George's coat was clear and his lilac points so defined. His eyes were like pools of crystal-clear sea water: so blue, so beautiful. I did make one mistake, however: when I would leave for work, I would watch George watching me, and I thought to myself how sad he looked, being left alone all day awaiting my return. WRONG! George was perfectly happy. How silly was I to think differently!

George grabbed a piece of my soul—some would say he was my "heart cat." I referred to him as my feline soul mate. He was a character and he knew it. Even meeting actors from the Australian world of film and television didn't faze him. George felt they should have been honoured to meet him, not the other way around.

I arrived home from work one evening and went through my usual routine, which basically involved throwing my coat and handbag on the nearest hook and picking George up. But I noticed that this time something wasn't right. I recoiled in horror and looked again to see that George's balance was all over the place. NO! Absolutely NO! Not my George! He is indestructible! The fear resonated through me, regurgitating all the feelings when I'd lost Oliver all those years previously. I grabbed the phone and demanded the emergency vet attend my home, and no, I wasn't the slightest bit interested in the receptionist telling me there would be an out-of-hours charge. How could she be so insensitive? This was George!

The vet arrived quite quickly and pried George from my arms. I had totally convinced myself that it was a stroke. But to my surprise the vet believed that George had an inner ear disorder resembling labyrinthitis in humans. He would need an operation. The next thing I saw was the vet's car disappearing into the distance, carrying my precious boy: the most precious cargo she would ever transport. I was left in stunned disbelief.

The following day the vet phoned to say that George had come through his operation, but only time would tell if he would still be able to hear. But I wasn't listening—my George was okay! Of course he was—he was George. I immediately booked time off from work and spent the next three days visiting George at the veterinary hospital. The vet and their nurses knew it was absolutely pointless to even attempt to tell me there were set visiting hours! I hand-fed him both his recovery food and, to his delight, some tinned tuna, which he tucked into. On the third day, the vet said I could take him home, but not before presenting me with a rather unpleasant looking bill! I settled it and swept George into my arms, where he purred quite happily.

With George all healed, and with full hearing, he and I were back together. This had given me a huge wake-up call that one day we would not be so fortunate. I needed to prepare myself for whenever that might occur. No matter how I tried to push the inner voice away, it was there; it would show up every so often, like some sort of inner warning bell. This continued intermittently for three years after that operation.

One day I noticed George seemed a little under the weather. I monitored him for a couple of days, and he perked up. I thought that, like any of us, maybe he'd just felt a bit out of sorts. But once again the inner voice came back, forcing me to take George to the vet for a check-up. And this time the voice would not be silenced.

George and I were the only ones in the waiting room. The vet came through and said, "Well, then, young man, let's have a look at you." George obligingly hopped onto the table in the consultation room. The vet smiled and said, "If only all cats were so obedient..." George looked at him as if to say, "All cats, are not me, Mr. Vet!" The vet examined George thoroughly, and upon feeling his abdominal area, he asked if I would permit a further scan. When I asked why, the vet said that he just wanted to check something further, so I consented.

The vet returned, showed me the scan, circled a small area, and said, "Hazel, I hope this isn't what I think it is. But whatever it is, it needs to come out now, before it gets larger." I questioned what he thought and got the news I didn't want to hear: he believed it was the start of a liver tumour. I looked at George, who by that time was chasing a fly around the waiting room, and my heart jumped into my throat. I knew, however, what had to be done, and the operation was booked for September 3, 2009. The day before—and don't ask me what prompted me to do this—I got my camcorder out and recorded George playing.

On the day of surgery, I begged the vet to promise me I'd get George back, which was of course thoroughly unfair on my part. The vet knew what George meant to me. After kissing George on the head goodness knows how many times, I returned home and occupied the agonising time by cleaning my home from top to bottom, anything to distract me from a call I never wanted to receive.

At precisely midday the vet phoned. "Hazel, it's me. I...I'm so very sorry, but George didn't make it. The tumour was far larger than

I'd envisaged, and I'm not even sure I got it all out. I did my best, but he died coming around from the anaesthetic. I'm so sorry!" He then went on, "Would you like to come and see him?" I broke down. My feline soul mate was gone. I was completely alone. My home is small, but it suddenly felt cavernous. I was devastated.

A friend of mine who used to work in cat rescue accompanied me to the vet's surgery, and there was George lying on the table, looking so peaceful—honestly, he just looked asleep. I wrapped my arms around him and cried, "Baby, please wake up, come back to Mummy, for goodness sakes, please!" The vet came through, shaking his head. I could see that he too had been crying. He said, "Hazel, if it's any consolation, in my whole career I have never seen such a seriously ill cat look so beautifully healthy. His coat is amazing—he's a credit to you".

The vet went on to explain that the dot he'd seen on the scan was the top of a very large liver tumour. To be honest, the man probably said a whole lot more to me, but my brain wasn't processing. I stated there and then that never ever again would I ever have another animal in my life, for there could never, and would never, be another George. The vet looked at my friend, and I do remember him saying, "Once the shock of this has settled, please try and convince Hazel differently, because if all the animals I see were this loved, my job would be so much easier." I glared at the vet, not wanting to accept his compliment—then suddenly I felt an overwhelming anger surge through me. Thankfully, the thoughts remained within me, as it would have been very unfair for me to vocalise them through high emotion. Burning inside of me were questions such as "WHY DID YOU NOT SAVE GEORGE?! YOU CHARGE A FORTUNE AT THE BEST OF TIMES! DID YOU NOT STUDY TO BECOME A DOCTOR OF VETERINARY MEDICINE FOR YEARS? CLEARLY, YOU LEARNED NOTHING!" These sorts of questions rolled around and around in my head like a marble in a tin for weeks.

Arriving home, putting my key in the front door, and walking in alone was hideous. I didn't want anyone with me. My little house was still, cold, and unwelcoming. I wandered around, talking into thin air, "What am I going to do without you in my life? You meant the world to me and you knew it!"

A song by Phil Collins entitled "Against All Odds" was playing on the neighbour's radio. The words of the chorus were so fitting that I froze. It was as if my soul was talking to George:

"So take a look at me now

Well there's just an empty space

And there's nothing left here to remind me

Just the memory of your face

Ooh take a look at me now

Well there's just an empty space

And you coming back to me is against the odds

And that's what I've got to face"

The lyrics of the next verse compounded matters:

"I wish I could just make you turn around

Turn around and see me cry

There's so much I need to say to you

So many reasons why

You're the only one who really knew me at all"

The following day, I learned that, due to the economic climate, I was to lose my job in the international property sector. I was dealing with what to me was a colossal bereavement, and now I was given the news that I would shortly be without income at all. Having nobody and nowhere to turn, I now had the fight of my life on my hands: to try to secure new employment and in doing so save the roof over my head, and, on top of that, to grieve.

But who cares when it comes to animal bereavement, right?!

I did find alternative employment eventually of course, and in the interim my social life was utilised organising voluntary events, which occupied my mind. In hindsight, I was probably occupied too much, as distraction is not always the best way to deal with grief. Nonetheless, the events went off seamlessly, and without realising it I was spreading myself emotionally too thin. This was to take its toll over not just the immediate days and weeks after George's passing, but for months and years to come. I was, however, adamant that my love would never be shared with another four-legged friend. George had taken it all, and quite rightly, with him. The consequence to this was emotional stagnation.

People talk of "signs" from your beloved animal after they have gone to Rainbow Bridge. If only I'd have not been so deeply consumed with grief, I'd have spotted them. Approximately three months after George's passing, driving home on a dark, rainy November night, with tears complementing the weather, I arrived home. My car headlights picked up what looked like a parcel on my front doorstep. Great, I thought, that silly courier has left a delivery for me, out in this weather. Some people are clueless!

I paused, realising that I'd not ordered anything, so I got out of my car to see what it was. The object moved, and the deepest orange eyes, set into fur as black as the night sky, stared back at me in a most pronounced way. Since George had gone, I couldn't bring myself to look at a photo of another cat, let alone see a real one. The tears started, and I slowly moved towards this little being. It stood up. I say "it," which I don't like to use—but it could have been a he or a she, I will never know.

I unlocked my front door; the cat invited itself in before I could do anything to stop it and boldly took itself around the house. It wandered around the downstairs before heading upstairs. My home isn't large, so this took maybe a minute or two, though it felt longer. I remember not really being able to move, like I was frozen to the spot. Then, as quick as it had arrived, the cat, seeing the front door still ajar, disappeared. Immediately concerned for its welfare, I tried to follow it. Memories of Oliver flew into my head. I couldn't let this little one suffer a similar fate on such a miserable night. However, I couldn't find it. I looked, but nothing. I'd never have missed such deep orange eyes staring back at me, regardless of the dark and the rain—but it had simply vanished. I started to question if I'd imagined everything. All felt quite surreal.

The following morning while standing to drink a hot mug of tea, I clearly remember looking at the clock on the oven: 11:11. I recalled the events from the previous night and suddenly wondered how I would react if a neighbour's cat came into my garden after all these weeks. I walked, holding my mug, from the kitchen to the lounge, and there, in my garden, staring back at me, was a very large tabby and white cat. GEORGE! What are you trying to tell me? Okay, this time I knew the cat—it belonged to a neighbour—but he had never ever ventured into my garden.

I fought the feeling of even looking for another kitten, but something inside of me kept telling me to start researching British Shorthair breeders. I did, with trepidation and many tears, and found one located about 45 minutes from my home. I contacted her and met her many times over several months. The first time, I couldn't bring myself to even look at another British Shorthair, let alone contemplate taking one home. I even saw a litter being born—new, beautiful babies—but no, I shook my head, I can't.

June 2010 would be a transformation for me. Eight months had passed, and I was almost getting used to my home simply being a house: it was soulless, and I just didn't want to be in it much. The breeder had invited me over for dinner and told me that she had a litter upstairs born a few days earlier. Sadly, two had been born asleep; the ones who had survived were three girls and one boy—a big lad and the eldest. I realised from what the breeder was saying that the colouration of the parents of this litter matched exactly that of George's parents. I found myself enquiring as to the pedigree and was shown. Distantly, oh so very distantly, I spotted a prefix I recognised—it was the same as George's! There was a connection!

I went to see them, bent down, stroked the boy, and blurted out, "Please, can I have the cream pointed boy?!" Even though he was still pure white, I knew he'd be cream, just like his father. The breeder looked at me, and to be honest I think my expression was that of surprised shock. I'd not been expecting to say that, and she wasn't expecting it either, so she told me to take some time to think about it. This wasn't what I wanted to hear. That evening, after a very nice meal and catch up, I drove home feeling a sense of hope, positive that he was and had to be MY boy. This little kitten would be my "soul plaster," a Band-Aid to me from George and Oliver so I could heal.

I rang the following day, and the breeder told me that another breeder had enquired after him as a future stud cat. I went cold. No, that could not happen. I think the breeder could tell what this meant to me; she asked me to give her a little time to think. About an hour later, my phone rang and I was invited back over. The breeder, quite rightly, wanted to know whichever home she chose would be right. She asked so many questions. I don't remember even half of the answers I gave, but they must have been agreeable, as I got the news that she would be more than happy for him to go to a "pet" home.

But there was a fly in the ointment: I had booked to go to Australia on holiday, and, as you can't have a pedigree kitten until it's 13 weeks old, this little boy would be older than that by the time I returned to the UK. I froze, hoping this wouldn't change her mind. It didn't; she said she'd hang onto him for me and asked me if I'd thought of a name. Oh yes, I had! He would be Hugo: an acronym standing for "Hazel United (with) George and Oliver." But very few people would know this; it would be our secret.

The whole time I was in Australia, I could think of nothing other than him. The visit over there wasn't particularly enjoyable, and eventually, six weeks later I arrived home after a very long direct flight. Walking through the door, that cold, empty feeling hit me: my house without a soul. It had been this way for 13 months by this stage, and simply had to change.

I rang the breeder. Thankfully, I don't usually suffer too badly from jet lag, but she refused to allow me to drive over to her home, collect Hugo, and drive back. She said I needed to rest after such a long journey. She was right, and another endless 48 hours passed. Finally, the day arrived, October 18, 2010, when I could collect him! As I was driving over, I kept swirling the October 18 date around and around in my head, until I realised that it was the exact day back in 1996 when I had brought George home!

Hugo had of course grown immensely whilst I'd been away and was now a handsome 20-week-old boy. I walked upstairs and he, along with his sisters, came running to the breeder, who bent down and picked him up. I felt a bit guilty moving him from all he'd known, but the breeder assured me I was doing the best for him. As she handed him to me, Hugo nuzzled into my neck, purring like a train. I fought the tears and bit the bottom of my lip so hard I could taste blood, but I was determined I wouldn't worry him with my emotions. All that was needed was for him to have his microchip, the handing over of paperwork, the checking to make sure he was safe and secure in his carry case (which had a personalised blanket inside)—and off we drove home. Hugo never uttered a single noise the whole journey home.

Upon arrival, I opened the front door, and a warmth hit me as I placed Hugo's carry case on the hall floor. My home had instantly regained its soul. I opened the door, Hugo walked out, blinked at me, went into the lounge, jumped onto the armchair, curled up, and went to sleep. He was home, I was home. We were home together. That night, with Hugo curled up on my bed, George appeared in my dream for the first time in months. He too was curled up asleep. Hugo was most definitely meant to be.

And so, up until July 2020 this is how it was. Hugo was subsequently joined by another British Shorthair called Henry and a British Longhair called Heidi. This was my family. Everyone marvelled at how harmoniously the three cats got on. Hugo was the even-tempered, loyal, gentle giant. Absolutely nothing fazed him in life; he accepted it for what it was. He greeted everyone who visited and, when possible, investigated the contents of handbags in case there was a nice treat just for him!

The year is now 2020, quite literally, as described by most people I meet, "the year from hell." I don't know of many people whose lives haven't been affected by it. COVID-19 has been the dominant feature, but the whole year has been one which will surely go down in the history books: from ridiculously warm winter temperatures to indescribable rainfall and floods in February, followed then by the deadly coronavirus sweeping the world. For me, it is memorable for all the wrong reasons. The year, I would so unexpectedly be forced to say goodbye to Hugo. I still can't believe I am typing these words.

On the morning of July 6, I awoke because I heard neighbouring cats outside bellowing at each other. At first in my half-awake stupor I thought it was Henry and Heidi, as sometimes they tease each other, but no, it didn't sound like them. It was 5:40 a.m., and despite it being July, it was chilly. Hugo was on my bed, fast asleep (or so I thought). I stroked him, saying something like "Nothing fazes you, does it, Hewg?" I checked on Henry and Heidi: they looked a bit startled but were fine. Stroking Hugo again, not wanting to wake him (ironic as it turned out), I went to get back into bed. Something inside of me told me to check Hugo…

My beautiful, gentle boy, my Hugo, my special boy, had passed away in his sleep on my bed. He was still warm. I swept him up in my arms and just knew he had gone in his sleep—he had gone. Hugo had lived his life pleasing me, and he even saved me the trauma of having to say goodbye to him, as some people must, across a veterinary table. But I was in shock. Immediate memories of the night before began flooding my head. Hugo had been fine: he'd greeted me from work, played in the garden for a short time with Henry, Heidi, and me, and eaten all of his dinner. There were no signs that the following day I would be saying goodbye to him.

I grabbed a soft bath towel from the airing cupboard, swaddled him like a baby, and got down to the emergency veterinary hospital as fast as I could. The journey seemed eternal. Because of coronavirus, I had to meet the veterinary nurse in the car park. I said my goodbyes and thanks to my beautiful boy, which the kindly nurse allowed me to do privately, albeit at around 6:30 a.m. in a cold car park with a very shocked and broken heart. I handed him over to the nurse, pleading with her to bring him back to me, but she just looked at me and shook her head. Hugo had gone to sleep and simply not woken up.

Now of course I've had people tell me that this was a "lovely way for him to go," but I felt cheated for him as much as for myself. Hugo had had his 10th birthday only the month before. I turned myself inside out with grief, convincing myself I somehow had to be guilty:

flashbacks, my head regurgitating every recent memory of him. Had I missed something? This has to be your fault, Hazel. I didn't eat for four days and cried every single day for 64 days in succession, just as I'm crying reliving everything now. Hugo never asked for anything and gave me so much in return.

The first night after Hugo's passing, the silhouette of a cat, quite clearly Hugo, appeared in my dream, walking across the flowerbeds and to my lounge door. Naturally, I awoke in tears. The next couple of days passed uneventfully but in a bit of a blur. Day five at around three in the morning I awoke to my Alexa blaring a song I'd never heard before, let alone could have asked for. The song was entitled "Thank you for Loving Me." I didn't hear the full lyrics, just this one line. I turned Alexa off, sat in complete silence, and said, "No, Hugo, the thanks are all mine." Later that day I googled who sang this song and learned it was Bon Jovi.

That same week, I had a butterfly land in my garden on a potted plant, and it even allowed me to get close enough to take a really nice photo. This has happened several times since. I believe I've been blessed to see so many signs—and I can only but urge you all to look for signs from your beloved animal.

And I am so fortunate to have Henry and Heidi—they and I are slowly healing each other, because we all miss Hugo.

Now, midway through September, I have chosen to write the story of my boys to help heal me and to allow them to rest at Rainbow Bridge. Hugo's unexpected passing has most definitely reawakened memories of both George and Oliver. I am reconciling with myself, albeit slowly, that none of my beautiful boys would wish me to be like this.

Since 1989 I have been privileged to have had these special boys in my life. Their passing has taught me a number of lessons, but primarily, not to rush grief simply to please others. The more you try to push grief away, the more it will push back. Grief is not an illness, but the cure, if that's even the right word, is to take time, to be patient with oneself, and to cry. I believe crying cleanses and it's healing. Whilst no two people are the same, if you can find others to truly empathise, then share stories and keep memories alive. The tears are the small price we pay for years of unconditional love and loyalty, in my opinion.

I read something recently which said that our animals may not be our whole lives because we have our work, family, and friends. However, we are theirs. They spend their little lives waiting for us to return home so that they can shower us with a friendship which is the epitome of trust. I agree.

We can tell our animals our happiest moments or our deepest secrets—they are like miniature therapists. The fact that we mourn for them when they pass is our testament to the love we will have for them for the rest of our lives. None of our four-legged family members would wish to see us perpetually in mourning. It's all about finding the balance within oneself and slowly returning to an adjusted way of life. Some people will never understand, and we then have to encounter those stereotypical questions which I need not detail, for we all know what they are. I have an element of pity for these people who have never themselves experienced the special unbreakable bond that any animal lover has.

Oliver, George, and Hugo, my eternal love and thanks to you all. I have truly been so lucky, maybe more than I ever deserve, but I will keep you in my heart until we meet again.

CHAPTER 8

❧

CELEBRATING OUR PETS

"There's a bit of magic in everything, and some loss to even things out." ~ Lou Reed, 'Magic And Loss'

Some of our contributors chose to focus their stories not on the circumstances of their losses but on happy memories from their pets' lives. Darlene treasures her memories of happy times with Biscuit and Quincey. Janet was not Pirate Cat's mom, yet she still learned valuable lessons from him about acceptance and love. Denise is grateful to Show Me Jack for his uncanny ability to sense exactly what she needed as she went through a very difficult time of her life. And Ji salutes Leonard, who in just four short years taught her so much, including to enjoy life to the fullest.

I'm sure you've noticed that a common theme that keeps coming up in these stories is how our pets love us so freely and unconditionally. I would suggest that the best way to honor the memory of those who have gone to the Rainbow Bridge is precisely to share that same kind of love with all the other animals and people in our lives.

BISCUIT
BY DARLENE

Biscuit

I got Biscuit when he was five months old from a friend who was unable to keep him for a variety of reasons. I went to meet him and fell totally in love: he was an adorable fluffy white Maltipoo with beautiful brown eyes. As soon as I looked into those eyes and he looked at me, our souls connected. It was perfect timing to bring a fur baby into our lives: I was retiring and my husband was retired already. I couldn't wait for my husband to meet him. Needless to say, he fell in love with Biscuit also.

Biscuit turned into a momma's boy quite quickly—he never wanted me out of his sight. On our walks he would walk in front of me, but always looked back to make sure I was there with him. He also loved for me to carry him, which I would do at times just to get his snuggles against my face and his little whiskers against my cheek.

He loved to sit on my lap and hide his face under my elbow and sleep. Those were our special moments together.

Going on vacation was traumatic for both Biscuit and me. Although we had a great sitter that loved him and took great care of him, I had an awful time leaving him while we went away. He would cry when I would hand him to her, and I would cry also. The best part of vacation was when it was over and it was time to go get my boy—how happy we would be to see each other!

Biscuit's favorite toy was a small, furry, squeaky ducky. That was his go-to toy—no matter how many toys you bought him, the ducky was his favorite. He loved to grab and run with it so that I would chase him—that was our favorite playtime together. Another favorite game was when he would sneakily grab a throw pillow from the sofa and run with it, even though the pillow was bigger than him. He would take off running with it, then wait for me to chase him down—great exercise for both him and Momma. He loved to get on the bed in the mornings and roll around and stick his head under the pillows and hide his face, then pop out from under the pillow with his fur messy around his face and one ear flipped over. What a fun time he would have, and it would make us laugh.

His favorite snacks were doggie lean treats, and his favorite vegetables were green beans and sweet potatoes. He also loved his peanut butter snacks. He liked for me to stay by him while he ate his meals—he would always stop eating to look and make sure I was there beside him. Evenings at about 8:00 was snack time with his daddy, and he knew it too. No matter what Biscuit was doing, he stopped right around that time and sat in front of his daddy to let him know that it was time for them to have their snack. That was their special time together.

Biscuit loved going on his walks several times a day. He loved seeing people and other doggies, although he was intimidated by larger dogs and would not go near them—he just barked at them from a distance. However, there was a beautiful golden retriever named Oscar that he absolutely loved, and when he would see Oscar coming down the street he would walk up to him and stand on his hind legs and lick Oscar's face. Oscar would just stand there and let him. And Oscar's daddy said that Biscuit was the only dog that Oscar would allow to do that.

We have a window seat, which was Biscuit's favorite place to hang out and watch people and other dogs walk by. He took naps there and would also sit there to watch for us to come home after running errands, etc. When we would pull up the driveway, he would jump out of that window so fast and be at the door waiting for us to come in so he could give us "glad you're home" kisses.

Biscuit loved our neighbor across the street from us. He would also watch for her to pull into her driveway, and, again, he would jump down from the window seat and run to our door to be let out so that he could see her. She would bring her two dogs out and they would hang out for a while. That was another highlight of his day. My neighbor would wave at him in the mornings when he was in the window and she was going to work. She loved our Biscuit boy.

I have learned so much from Biscuit: I have learned not to take life for granted, and to live in the moment. Love means everything. Biscuit made our lives brighter and gave us enormous joy and happiness. Love never dies.

Biscuit went to Rainbow Bridge at age 10 suddenly and unexpectedly one morning from a type of cancer called hemangiosarcoma which was never detected until it was too late. Needless to say, it broke our hearts. But I wanted his story to be about how he lived, not about how he left us—that's why I didn't go into all the details of that horrible day. I want to think about our happy times together and keep the happy memories in our hearts. I'd forgotten to mention that we had a bunch of other names for Biscuit: BBoy,

BabyB, Boo, Boo Boo, Mr.B, Momma's Boy, and Sunshine—I would always sing "You Are My Sunshine" to him. Because he was my sunshine for sure.

Writing Biscuit's story is an honor. It is what I needed to do, and what Biscuit would want me to do for him. We have so many precious memories of our boy, and he will be in our hearts forever. He knew he was loved, and we knew how much he loved us. We will be together one day, and what a joyful reunion that will be.

QUINCEY (BISCUIT'S KITTY BROTHER) BY DARLENE

Quincey

My sweet kitty Quincey came into our life when he was approximately one year old. Quincey was a handsome boy, black and white, and went by the name of Quin for short and also Kittyman and Mr. Quin. We had had a black and white cat that went to Rainbow Bridge a few months before my husband found Quincey hanging out in the warehouse at work. Every time my husband went into the warehouse, Quincey would jump from a shelf onto his shoulder.

My husband would come home each day and tell me about him. I knew he wanted to bring him home, so I gave in and let him. I think it was meant to be—such a precious, sweet kitty he was. He had the sweetest meow. Everyone loved him. He loved basking in the sun and jumping into boxes to sleep. He loved to give love bites, but sometimes he bit a little too hard. Quincey loved sitting in the window seat watching people walk by with their doggies, and loved chasing the lizards that got onto the screened room.

Quincey loved being around people. When company would come to our house, he wanted to lie across their feet or next to them on the sofa. He wasn't much for playing with toys, but he loved chasing a laser light. He loved to annoy his daddy by sitting right in the middle of anything my husband was trying to put together. He wanted to be daddy's little helper, but his daddy didn't see it that way.

Quincey loved his doggie brother Biscuit, who sadly went to Rainbow Bridge less than a year before Quincey. Quin and Biscuit got along so well. They loved chasing each other, and Quin would lie up on the sofa, just waiting for Biscuit to walk around the side of the sofa so he could swat him on the head. They would lie in the window seat together in the sunshine right next to each other. And both were content lying next to me on the sofa.

Oh, how I miss my boy. I miss his soft fur, his sweet, handsome face, and his sweet disposition. Sadly, Quincey went to Rainbow Bridge at the age of 17. He had kidney failure, and it seemed like it got worse after Biscuit was gone. I could tell he missed his doggie brother so much. I know they are together now, chasing each other and playing. They will both be there together waiting to greet their momma and daddy at Rainbow Bridge when the time is right. Quincey, we love and miss you. You will always be in our hearts.

THE TAIL (TALE) OF PIRATE CAT
BY JANET

Pirate Cat's Tail

I learned a great lesson about love and dedication to your passion and the people that you love from a scruffy orange and white street cat named Pirate Cat.

Pirate Cat was a formerly feral cat with a tipped left ear, indicating that he had been captured, neutered, and released. He came to be adopted from an animal shelter by his caregivers Amanda Cancilla and her boyfriend Matt Gufreda, who quickly learned that Pirate Cat was determined to be an outdoor cat. He tore up the floor and door that exited from their kitchen, but he did return home to eat, sleep, and get care and love after his brawls and adventures. He got the name Pirate Cat from his penchant for sitting on the shoulders of his caregivers, much like a pirate's parrot.

Near his home was a public access trail called the Monon Trail, converted from former railroad tracks that had been paved over. The trailhead had a parking lot and a rest area with benches, restrooms, and a water fountain that was equipped with a ground level bowl for pet use. This trailhead became Pirate Cat's domain, and he appeared there daily to get head pats, give leg rubs, and get drinks of water. He patrolled the immediate area, which included a business building and apartments.

 Pirate Cat achieved fame in 2017, when he was captured by the Indiana State Police and taken to a shelter. At that time there was a $150 fine for owning feral cats in one of the counties that was his territory. His Facebook page was created, the story hit the local televised news, and a local attorney offered to take his case pro bono. More and more people posted pictures of their encounters with Pirate Cat to his Facebook page, and his fame and popularity grew to 7500 followers.

 Pirate Cat became known as the Mayor of the Monon, a job he embraced, and as a skilled politician he continued his daily visits to greet his constituents and fans. Like any good politician, he was drawn to babies, women, and children, but readily approached anyone. He would seek out sips of water, preferring that they be served from the owner's water bottle, which became known as "drinking rum."

 Pirate Cat was hit by a car when crossing the street to get to the trailhead, but with no broken bones, he did not slow down and quickly returned to his duties. He was outfitted with a collar and tags containing his own phone number and a GPS locator so that maps of his adventures on the high seas could be posted to his Facebook page. His phone number went to a voice mail announcing that he was not lost and had a home. I followed him on Facebook and finally got to meet him in 2019.

 Then in April 2020 he went missing.

 His distinctive collar was found miles from the trailhead. Shelters were notified. Alerts went out to the public. The police were involved.

Days later, and near death, he was recovered. He lived long enough to be reunited with Amanda and Matt, but he had used the last of his nine lives to get home.

Thousands of fans were heartbroken and posted condolences and memories to his page.

What I learned from Pirate Cat is to remain true to your passion and never be afraid to share your love. He found his passion, which was to be with the people that he loved every day at his domain on the Monon Trail, and he moved heaven and earth to be there. He showed great courage in the face of many obstacles, and he always found a way to return to his post as Mayor of the Monon. I still am amazed at the number of lives that he touched and the hearts that he won during his time there. If a cat can show such courage and passion, can we not follow his lead and be kind to each other, accept all others as loveable, and never be afraid to share that love every day.

SHOW ME JACK
BY DENISE

Show Me Jack

Show Me Jack was from the line of Quarter Horses descended from the great stallion Two Eyed Jack. He was a copper penny red stallion and a gentle giant. He came into my life at a very difficult time and became my friend, my confidant, and my solace.

I was in therapy for childhood sexual abuse, and the sessions were grueling. I came out of the office spent, emotionally beat up, and with barely a hope that I would ever get through the therapy, much less heal.

A friend invited me to come as often as I liked to their Quarter Horse ranch of 35 acres just five minutes from my home. I had loved horses since I was little and had worked with them as an adult. Just smelling manure made me feel grounded. I said, "Can I come now?"

That is when I met Jack. I walked up to him and let my hands slide down his shiny neck, into his mane, and over his broad back as he nuzzled me. I had never seen a stallion so gentle and so red. Little did I know what he would come to mean to me.

I began to work with Jack, exercising him and grooming him. Jack would lope in a smooth rhythm that would mesmerize me into calm. I started coming almost every day, but especially on therapy days, which were often three days a week.

I started riding him bareback with only a bosal around his nose. Just a slight move of my leg, and he would do whatever I wanted. I would move him to the fence and climb up on his broad, smooth back, and the two of us would ride away. I felt like I was free from everything when I was galloping across the pasture with Jack. I had never known a horse like him. On the hard days, I would just mount him with nothing on him, take him to a pasture, and lie on his back and cry as he grazed. The smell of his coat, the feel of his powerful body beneath me, and the sun on my back comforted me and restored me. He seemed to know just what I needed and gave it to me. In this way, I got through many hard years of therapy and began to heal.

But then Jack got colic. With the vet, we did all we could—taking turns staying up all night, walking him, giving him medicine- -and 24 hours in, it looked like he had turned the corner and was going to make it. He stopped sweating, stomping, and was even drinking. But a few hours later, the colic took over with a vengeance. We knew that we would have to help him leave this world.

I cried as a bulldozer dug the huge hole where he would lie. I could not believe this was happening—none of us could. The vet came; I hugged my Jack for one last time and said I would see him on the other side someday. We walked him into the grave, the sedative was administered, and we watched him crumple to the ground. The medication to stop his gentle heart was given and he was gone.

That beautiful soul did more for me than I can ever describe in this short story. By the time he passed away, I was doing well and nearing the end of therapy. I will never forget him or his gifts to me or the way I felt on his back or by his side. He was and always will be "My Jack, My Heart."

LEONARD
BY JI

Leonard

Like many other sweet animals, Leonard had a hard beginning. He was found as a kitten at a construction site and turned in to my vet. He spent his first few months at the vet clinic, and everyone wanted to take him home, but the vet never let anyone have him. He was a little hellion, climbing up legs, sticking his nose into everything, teasing anything on two or four legs. The day I met him I thought he was adorable and picked him up. He settled down and let me carry him around. Everyone at the clinic looked at me strangely, and they told me he had never calmed down like that before. I took him home that day.

I've been blessed with so many special animals in my life, and Leonard is at the top of my list of blessings. There were a lot of things special about him. Leonard lived life wide open. There was nothing he didn't embrace fully, whether it was learning from one of the barn cats how to hunt rabbits, playing with a toy and jumping as high as my head, or trusting me like no one else ever has. He loved to learn and was clicker trained to sit, down, wait at doors, recall from as far as my barn, jump onto a perch like a circus lion, and so much more. He helped me train puppies. He loved going outside and smelling the grass and scratching on trees.

When Leonard was about two, he started having breathing issues. We ultimately discovered that he had a condition called hypertrophic cardiomyopathy. In other words, in one of those great ironies of life, his heart was growing too big. Sometimes I think he was trying to let his physical heart get as big as his emotional one. His prognosis from the cardiologist at the specialty clinic was not good, and not long, maybe a couple of months.

I went to the vet I got Leonard from and asked if we could set up hospice at home. I didn't want him to have to be locked in a crate at the specialty vet on a regular basis because of the problems that I knew were coming. My vet was amazing, and we set up his medications and an oxygen tent for him at home. His clicker training came in handy, and he gladly came running to jump up on his perch three times a day for his many pills and shots. In fact, despite the fact that I was giving him nine pills a day plus occasional injections, he would come get me and yell at me if I was a minute late for his medicine time. I swear he knew. When he finally got so sick that I had to take him back to the specialty clinic, they couldn't believe he was still alive. Their initial prognosis was about two months, and we were lucky enough to have him for almost two more years. The following is my goodbye letter after losing Leonard at only four years old.

Today Leonard, my dear friend and companion, finished his work in this life. There was an enormous soul traveling in that little furry package. I believe he wouldn't want me to be sad, but instead to remember him and be happy, to keep playing with puppies and reveling in the sunshine. So I made a list of just a few of the things Leonard taught me in his short time here:

He taught me the joy in sniffing dirt, tasting a blade of grass, and chasing butterflies.

He taught me that if you never hold a grudge, then you never have to worry about forgiving anyone.

He taught me that the best days are spent playing in the woods, but only if you have a warm family to come home to.

He taught me that some days you just need to stay in bed all morning.

He taught me that every day holds something wondrous and fascinating, and to always be curious about whatever life hands you.

He taught me that you can jump higher than anyone expects if you are motivated enough.

He taught me that profanity is better than violence, and most of the time you can avoid conflict by quietly holding your ground. I bet if he had been a human, he would have cursed like a sailor on shore leave.

He taught me that when you do fight, it's always best to end it by grooming the other guy's ears and paws to make everything right—even if you have to hold them down to do it.

He taught me that the best place to nap is in the middle of a pile of puppies, even if you are a cat.

He taught me that cats and dogs not only can get along but should.

He taught me that even though I can do something, that doesn't always mean I should. (I really need to remember that one.)

He taught me to unhesitatingly grab every moment of joy from life up to the last second.

Sleep well, my friend.

CHAPTER 9

❦

FREQUENTLY ASKED QUESTIONS ABOUT GRIEF

"Death leaves a heartache no one can heal, love leaves a memory no one can steal." ~ From a headstone in Ireland

L osing your beloved pet, no matter the circumstances, will undoubtedly conjure up a whole host of questions, leaving you wondering whether they are normal or typical. Please be reassured that you are not alone. Whilst this list of questions below is not exhaustive and may not contain every question you have, these are the most common. Most people will undoubtedly be able to relate to these.

Why did this happen to me?

Sadly, none of us knows what tomorrow may bring. There is no rhyme or reason for the things that happen in our lives. We all have a finite time on this earth, and no matter when the end of life comes, it is a day few choose to acknowledge voluntarily. Nobody can control the end of life. It is the most difficult of questions to answer as there is never a satisfactory reply, and if you are like me, you will always be looking for answers to a question that can never be answered.

What have I done wrong?

When we lose somebody that we love, we often experience the most common response—guilt. Did we do enough? Why didn't we do this or that? It's a constant battle within ourselves. Ultimately, however, **you have done nothing wrong**. After a loss occurs, it is so much easier to look back in hindsight and think we could have done something different. As pet owners, none of us goes around doing anything harmful or neglectful towards something that is so precious to us. Please be kind to yourself and recognize that, in fact, you did absolutely everything right for your friend. Your current emotions are testament to the love you had for each other. And please check out Chapter 3 for more about dealing with guilt.

How long will I feel like this?

Another very good and most natural of questions. It is said that grief never truly goes away; we just rebuild our lives around the sadness and adjust to a new normality. You heal around the wound. You become bigger than the grief. There will be days where you feel as though life is slowly returning to your usual routine, but there will also be bumps in the road when a trigger, such as a memory, a song, or a picture will provoke an intense emotional reaction. All of this is to be expected. As time progresses, your life will adjust. It's not a case of "time healing all wounds"—merely that with the passage of time, you rebuild around it and eventually accept it, even though it may be a reluctant acceptance. Remember, there is no time limit on grief. It is important that you take your time so that you heal.

Could I have done more?

Ask yourself this question again, albeit a bit more slowly: "Could...I...have...done...more?" Well, if you could have, you absolutely would have. Of course you know this intellectually, but grief is making you question the final weeks, final days, final hours and minutes. Your pet was ultimately so happy with your home and your life that they would answer that you did absolutely everything possible. It is so easy to look back and wonder if you could have done anything more. Be proud of the fact you gave your dearest friend the absolute best life that you could.

Will I ever be happy again?

The answer is quite simply yes. You will find happiness again. Healing within yourself takes time, and unfortunately society doesn't always make allowances when it comes to non-human family members. Try not to allow yourself to be pressured into conforming to what society expects, and allow yourself some deserved patience and healing as you adjust to a new normality for you. With each passing day, you will become a little stronger as you evolve around the loss of someone you loved so much. Keep believing in yourself and the fact that you will be happy once more. Fill yourself with joyous memories of the wonderful times you spent with the one you loved, knowing you carry them with you forever in your heart. Love prevails over everything.

Why am I dreading the approaching holiday season so much?

Holiday times are undoubtedly some of the roughest to navigate, because they are expected to be full of love, enjoyment, and pleasure: we can come together to spend time with our loved ones and people whom we may not see from one year to the next. The anticipation of the holidays can leave us overwhelmed with feelings of pain, anger, and dread. Our pets are part of our family unit, and now there is a member of that unit conspicuous by their absence. You will undoubtedly hear your inner voice saying things like, "This time last year he/she was still here…" But now you feel like you have to comply with expectation of society that you should eat, drink, and be merry, when in truth you couldn't be feeling less sociable if you tried. This is to be expected. You might also tell yourself that if you show any signs of unhappiness, you will somehow cast a cloud over other people's fun. This is perfectly understandable, and as a matter of fact is the precise reason you are dreading the approaching festivities. If you can, try to calmly explain that you wish everyone all the enjoyment in the world, but ask them to be considerate towards your feelings at present. Remember, it is okay to say no to invitations. Don't take on too much. Start a new ritual to honour your beloved. If you go to visit family and friends, have an exit plan in place if things become too much for you. Be gentle with yourself and always look after you.

Why can't my family and friends truly understand my grief?

Grief is so personal, so individual, and even two people living in the same household may have differing ways of dealing with it. And because we live in a grief-illiterate society, it's certainly true that there are people who simply cannot understand and who may act in a way which you feel is insensitive to your needs. For example, if your friends have never enjoyed the love that an animal brings into our lives, they will struggle to comprehend the depth of your grief. Try not to unburden yourself to those whose replies may seem dismissive simply through their lack of true understanding. On the other hand, if the animal who has passed away was within your household, maybe your partner or family members are trying to reconcile their own grief and simply don't have the energy resources available to absorb yours as well. Communication, space, and time can be the best healers in such situations. It is so important not to make expectations of people who just cannot fill you with what you need. Find your tribe—people who can relate to what you are going though. If you go to my website https://petsorrow.com , I have a lot of ways in which you can connect with me. We have a newsletter and a loving Facebook group.

I feel so guilty, and I can't get this thought out of my head. What should I do?

Of all the emotions people endure after a loss, guilt is one of the biggies. I've dedicated Chapter 3 of this book to guilt for just this reason. No matter what happened in the loss of our pet, you will likely feel some sort of guilt. It is a natural response. When something goes wrong, we try to figure out why. We look for answers to questions we can never answer. We blame ourselves. We think we had control over the situation, but none of us has that power. Think of how miserable our pets would be if we wrapped them up so that they would be safe and protected from everything. With all things in life there is risk involved. Every time we get in our cars or jump on a plane, something could happen to us. We have no control over our destiny or anyone else's. It is important for guilt to be worked through so that you can move forward in a healthy manner.

Why do I feel so low when I hear clichéd statements that are supposed to cheer me up?

We live in a largely grief-illiterate society. But remember that very few people will say anything to deliberately cause further pain and upset. Their messages and statements often aren't comforting to you because your heart is broken, and what they're saying doesn't specifically relate to how you're feeling at that moment. In your mind, the platitudes may seem trivial and belittling to the unique relationship you had with your pet. And of course you are highly likely to hear the tired and worn-out comments such as "It was only a dog/cat/horse/bird..." which make you wince, as there was nothing "only" about the someone who you loved so much. As a defence mechanism, we become afraid to say anything for fear of hearing statements that seem uncaring. Friends and family who reply to your fragile words with remarks such as "Oh, don't worry, you can always get another" are folks who are not seeing your pet as you did and still do. To you, your animal was your friend, your confidant, your equal. These individuals may believe it is their way of offering advice when they don't know what else to say at such a delicate time. Even though the intent of the words is meant to be positive and said with care, you interpret them as hollow and standardised. This is where you need to gather up your remaining strength and let certain words roll off you like water off a duck's back. I like to believe that people mean the best, but sometimes they just say the wrong things. Don't disklike them because of this.

I feel my grief is taking too long to heal and I'm being judged. How should I respond?

Let me just reassure you that there is NO time limit on grief just because society wants us to get back to normal! You need time to grieve—**lots** of time. People need to comprehend that you are mourning the loss of a family member, and grief does not come with a calendar. If you rush yourself through this time of distress, any and all subsequent bereavements are highly likely to end up being compounded further by drawing on the suppressed grief. A visible wound needs time to heal—and so does an invisible one. It takes time for your heart and head to agree upon what has happened. Never compare how you are grieving to anyone else. All grief is unique, just like we are all unique as individuals. When you focus on how others are seeing you, you are out of your head and into theirs. Just focus on you. But if you ever feel that your grief is just too much, remember no book or Facebook group can ever replace professional help.

How do I get the images of his/her last days out of my head so I can move forward and think of only the good times?

This is the advice I give to people who come to see me at my clinical office. When you have an image in your conscious mind that is replaying over and over again, say the word "STOP!" Visualise a stop sign in front of you and immediately start thinking of a different picture. Maybe grab your cell phone and start looking at different images of happy times. When you shift your focus to something else, you interrupt the thought patterns you are going through, and your brain will begin to focus on something more positive. Practice makes perfect. You may have to do this a lot before the old negative memories begin to dissipate.

Due to the COVID-19 pandemic I had to hand my pet over to a veterinary professional in their car park. How can I ever forgive myself when the animal I lost meant so much more than that to me?

I am so sorry. I can't even imagine how awful and truly heartbreaking that must have been. Unfortunately, the COVID-19 pandemic is the new reality at the moment—unprecedented and completely beyond your control. You did nothing wrong; your decision was forced and out of your hands. Circumstances dictated that you had to comply with something you didn't want. Neither you nor the veterinary professional would have wanted this, but ultimately and in the cruellest of times you still did everything within your power for the animal you loved so dearly. Be gentle on yourself, and reconcile that there was absolutely nothing you could have done differently. You were still with your pet until the absolute final moment, and that is something no one can take away from you.

I loved my pet more than anything, yet I couldn't bring msyelf to stay with them in their final moments. How can I forgive myself?

During their lifetime, you did everything you could to be the best owner you were possibly able to be. The fact you were unable to stay with them at the end of their life does not make you a bad owner. It's not an easy thing to do—it's traumatic. It could quite simply be that you wanted to remember your pet as they once were, healthy and full of a zest for life. That's being human, not being a bad owner. You loved them dearly, and that's what matters. You must forgive yourself. Love lives on in your heart—and no one can ever take that away from you. Try not to focus on the negative—your pet knew they were loved right up to their last breath, and that I can promise you.

Why do I still cry when I try to talk about my loss?

The lyrics of the song "Missing Me" by RJ Helton say that you need to cry a thousand tears. What this means is that you need to release the emotions from your system as often as is necessary for you. Research has shown that crying releases oxytocin and endorphins which help us to deal with the pain. Never feel guilty for crying—crying is good and healing. If you suppress your tears, it will prolong your grief. The worst thing you can do is stuff your feelings down. Remember that each tear you cry shows the depth of love you had for your beloved. It's an accolade of you as the owner.

My animal was my soulmate. Our connection was so strong, and I've never felt such love. How can I possibly move forward?

There is not an easy answer to this exceptionally difficult question. Moving forward is very hard, and you can only move forward as fast as your heart allows you to heal. It's going to take time: grief is a process of emotions and time. You will never forget about that special soul, and I promise you that the love never goes away. That unique connection will remain with you throughout your life and lives on within your heart. You will feel love and light again, in time.

I believe my animal is with me in spirit and, furthermore, I have seen many signs. My friends and family think I'm being foolish. How should I respond?

This question I love, because I absolutely and personally believe that signs exist. In my opinion, not everything in the world can be proven scientifically. Please don't allow non-believers to steal your thunder or cast aspersions on you. Not only do I believe that we are sent comforting signs, but I will say that I myself have received many signs and symbols—ironically, they seem to come when I'm feeling the lowest. From my perspective, it's like there's an energetic force that needs to comfort me. I believe, and if you do, then in my opinion that's all that matters. Allow others to have their opinions, but accept that yours is different and be at peace within yourself for feeling the way you do.

People ask me if I'm going to replace my pet, as if they were a household appliance. This makes me angry. Am I wrong to feel this way?

In time, as your grief slowly begins to subside, only you will know if or when the time is right to open your heart to another animal. It is not for anyone else to suggest differently. Society often does not understand the depth of love we have for our pets, and unless you are an animal lover, that understanding cannot possibly be there. Some people think that by bringing a new life into yours it will give you a new focus and help with your pain. But unless the time is right, this wouldn't be fair on either you or another animal. There is no rule or guideline as to when the right time may be—it is simply a case of listening to your inner emotions and your heart. My wish is that one day another little life will be in yours, one that you can nurture, love, and enjoy.

I love animals, but the fear of going through this pain again is scaring me. Am I being silly?

No, you're not being silly—quite the reverse: you are responsibly considering the whole scenario. There is so much pain involved in loss that when you get to the point that you feel semi-whole again and might be leaning towards adopting another animal, I can totally understand how you might feel. To my way of thinking, the emptiness in our lives is so much bigger than the pain death brings, and nothing in comparison to the love we feel when we have them, which is unfailing and complete. Ask yourself if you can truly imagine never having an animal again and never having the loving friendship each one brings into our life. That connection is unique and offers so much. Don't be afraid to open your heart once more—as such a loving human being, you're unlikely to regret it. You will most definitely know if and when the time is right.

It's been almost three weeks now since my best friend passed away. I keep being told I shouuld be over the emotions by now but I'm not. What am I doing wrong?

Nothing—absolutely nothing wrong at all! Three weeks into a loss, you are still very much in what is termed the acute phase of grief. Emotions are raw, sensitivities are high. Please accept that you need to take time to process all the emotions being thrown at you. There is no blueprint to grief, and there is no timeline on it either. Nobody can tell you how long this will carry on. Furthermore, no one should be rushing you through your grief. You can't grieve in a wrong way. You are hurting from the pain of a broken heart, and healing after losing anything that you loved so much takes time. Lots of time.

I feel so much envy when I see other people with their pets. Am I being unfeeling?

Not at all, you're being human! It's natural to see other people with their pets and think, why can that not still be me? You're not wishing other people any distress, and ultimately, they will very sadly one day be feeling as you are. Know they are enjoying the same joy you once did and that their lives too are blessed by the love of an animal. The feelings you have are temporary, and it is grief's tight grip around your emotions making you realise what has gone from your life. Please don't be so hard on yourself as to consider yourself as unfeeling—you're simply missing the same companionship.

Why do I feel guilty if I have a day when I don't cry?

There's no need to feel guilty. Healing happens to every griever at different rates; there is no right and wrong to this. If the pet you lost was elderly, you may have begun your cycle of grief without realising it whilst they were still alive, as you subconsciously accepted that their time on earth was coming to an end. It could also be that you are surprising yourself by accepting the new normal that is happening in your life. Grief is unpredictable: you think all is going along okay and then a wave of emotion comes from out of nowhere and passes just as quickly. Nothing will ever erase the love you had for your pet, and you know within yourself that they would not want you to be constantly upset. Be kind to yourself, and accept that we all have our different ways of coming to terms with the loss.

My other pet(s) are grieving, and I'm grieving. How can I help them whilst helping myself?

This is such a wonderful question and one so seldom answered. Unfortunately, when one pet dies, leaving its companions behind as well as the grieving owner, the remaining pets are sometimes inadvertently and temporarily forgotten whilst the owner comes to terms with the loss. This is not a poor reflection of the owner—it's what grief, which is a very selfish emotion, does to us. From my perspective, the best answer I can give to this question is teamwork. You and your remaining pet(s) will become a stronger, more united team, helping each other to get through each new day. It will undoubtedly upset you to see your other animal(s) grieving, perhaps pacing around calling for their friend who will not be returning, so whenever possible try and remain as upbeat around them as you possibly can. Animals are so intuitive; they don't want you to be upset whilst trying to process their own feelings as to what has happened to their buddy. By being there for one another, and with the remaining pet(s) not passing judgement on your emotions or questioning your grief, you will work through the loss together. Play with them to distract them, as their little quirks and antics will undoubtedly make you smile even when you feel so low. Engage in more of the fun activities your remaining pet(s) love to do, and reward them because this will also make you feel good. Of course, if you're really worried about your remaining pet(s), then speak to your veterinarian.

I can't bring myself to put my pet's items away. Should I keep them or donate them?

There is no right or wrong answer to this question—it is most definitely your personal decision as to what you feel is appropriate. I remember when I brought Stelly (my second dog) home—I was very protective of Stella's items, and I watched them like a hawk so that they would not get wrecked. I did not want anything to happen to them. Initially, you may understandably wish to retain everything, then later maybe keep only items which were super special—for example, their collar or their blanket. You certainly shouldn't feel abnormal in any way if you want to keep everything which was theirs as their lasting legacy. Or you may decide to choose a small local charity or shelter that would be overjoyed to receive the items, which could make you feel good about helping an animal less fortunate than yours was. If you have other animals in your household, you may decide to keep their friend's items around them to reassure them. I have friends who have done this, and they say it works very well. Take your time with this decision, and whatever you decide will be the right answer. For myself, I kept all of Stella's things. I have her collar attached to the blinker bar in my car. I have all her toys, bed, and dog dishes—I just held onto them and passed them down to Stelly.

What signs do they send us?

I enjoy receiving this question, because I fervently believe that our adored pets do send us signs letting us know they are near—often when we least expect it. I've heard and also personally witnessed all manner of things, including birds, butterflies following people around, feathers suddenly appearing, getting a whiff of a smell associated with the pet, and hearing sounds that they might make. We can be fast asleep and suddenly feel an animal jump onto the bed, momentarily forgetting that the animal in question passed away maybe days, weeks, months or even years earlier. A visitation in one's sleep is a frequent occurrence; it happens at a time when we are resting, allowing our mind the freedom to accept the signs showing us all is well in their new realm. A friend of mine was awoken in the early hours of the morning just a few days after the loss of her adored cat to hear a song she'd never heard before, entitled "Thank You for Loving Me," playing on her Alexa. There was nobody else in her home; it was around 3:00 a.m., and since she'd never even heard of the song, the Alexa certainly wasn't requested to play it. I find such signs a real comfort at a time when we need it most. The day after I lost Stella, I received several amazing signs. The first was a huge white feather on a plastic box she would sit on every day—it was her perch. It greeted me as I made my way into work the next day. Then on my way home a beautiful rainbow appeared on a bright sunny day. It was another message from Stella, letting me know that she had crossed over. I will never forget it. I believe our loved ones do reach out to us in all sorts of ways. Be open to receiving the signs from them. In https://petsorrow.com/ under the Membership tab I have three audio downloads you can access for free—one of them is all about receiving signs from your loved one.

What are some positive steps I can take to help me move on?

Please refer to my Pet Sorrow website https://petsorrow.com , where you will find useful audio downloads and information in the members area. You are also invited to join the accompanying private Facebook group https://www.facebook.com/groups/healingsolutionsforpetloss where we take a deeper dive into understanding grief. In our compassionate group you are able to talk freely; your grief is validated and not judged. If you feel you need to do more and are still not progressing as much as you would like, then it may be worth obtaining professional counselling. Be mindful that as resourceful and productive as my website and group are—they have helped many grieving owners—they are not a substitute for more individualized and professional assistance.

CHAPTER 10

✑

PARTING THOUGHTS

"Nothing that grieves us can be called little; by the external laws of proportion a child's loss of a doll and a king's loss of a crown are events of the same size." ~ Mark Twain, 'Which Was The Dream?'

My goal in writing this book was to be for you the person that I did not have when I was broken down and full of grief.

Any time I have had a loss in my life, I needed to know WHY! Why did this have to happen to me, why didn't I do this, or why didn't I do that? So many whys! Whys with no answers. But because of my investigative mind and deep-rooted curiosity, I have always wanted to know as much as I can about any subject, even death.

I created this book to hopefully bring an understanding to your WHY. I truly believe that with proper comprehension anyone can build a house. My hope is that one day you will be able to build your house. And most importantly, find some of the answers to your whys.

Grief is a monster that takes hold of you and does not let you go until it is good and ready. Some days will be okay, other days will be awful, and you may even have days where you feel like you are going backwards.

Remember, there is no timeline or owner's manual for grief. As a griever, you have so much to go through, learn, feel, process, and come to terms with. It all takes time.

When you start to feel more happiness than anguish, you are well on your way to becoming healthier. And when you feel healthier, a new you will emerge. This is the part of the journey that most excites me, and it should excite you too. Who are you now? Things are different than they were yesterday, in so many ways, besides the obvious.

Now you may say to yourself, I don't want to be new—I want my life to be as it was. But you and I both know that you can never go back to being that individual. The loss of someone you love so much changes you. And life itself is always changing too. The road we travel on is full of ups and downs.

Think about this: in your lifetime you will never experience the same moment twice. Every day we live on this earth will be different from the day before. Every moment is different from the last moment. That is why it is so important to set up a gauge of some sort so you can look back and measure your growth.

The best way to do this is to journal. Journaling has so many benefits, plus it will serve as a measurement to see how you are doing. Writing down your thoughts and emotions reduces stress and keeps memories alive. It serves as a benchmark. We can go back and reread entries from the previous day, week, or month and now have something to measure against what we are feeling today. You will be able to see growth—and remember, even the smallest of accomplishments should be celebrated.

Now here is the thing: if you don't get into the practice of writing down every day how things are for you, it is harder to go back and try to recreate those feelings, emotions, and memories, because, boy, do they change moment to moment.

And this is a whole other rabbit hole we could go down, but I will touch on it briefly, because I want you to have answers to your whys. Have you ever tried to recall something from your past, and perhaps you tell your story to someone who was present at that time, and they have a different story than you—they remember something totally different?

How can that be? Both of you were there at the event, you both experienced the same thing, but your recollection of it is so different from your friend's.

Here is the reason why. Wait for a moment as I change my hat and cue the hypnotist in me to come out and explain to you how your mind works.

Our bodies and minds are made up of neurons, something on the order of 86 billion of them. The job of a neuron is to receive, process, and transmit information. When an event occurs, your brain determines what information is important and places that information in a file. The part of our brain that works with our memories is called the **hippocampus** (pronounced hih-puh-KAM-pus).

When we have a memory that we want to look back on, certain groups of neurons in our brain become re-activated. Now here is the interesting thing: research shows that when we go back and pull up a memory from our past, our recollection of that memory is only about half correct—even though we feel very confident that what we are recalling is 100 percent the way the event occurred.

It all has to do with how a memory gets stored in our brain. And every time we recall a memory, it has to go through a process in the retrieval of the memory, which is where things get changed up.

So let me take you back in time for a moment. Did you ever play that campfire game where you sit in a circle and whisper to the person beside you a short story—then that person whispers the story to the next person, and so on and so on. After the last person has the story whispered to them, they have to say it out loud—and the story is never the same as when it started out.

This is why it is so important for you to journal. Those precious moments and memories can then stay pretty similar to how you felt at the time, without the distortion that time puts on memories. Try to start your first entry the very first day when your life is forever changed. Your first alone day.

Now please don't despair if this is something you didn't do—it is never too late to start. Grab a notebook, buy a nice journal, or use your computer. Just begin to write about everything: how your day went, how many times you cried, how many times people said dumb things to you. Rate your sadness on a scale of 1 to 10. Did you have any moments of happiness? Write everything down.

Did you own a diary when you were little? I know I did—I can still see it in my mind. It was a pink Holly Hobbie diary with a lock on it. This little book became very special to me. It was a place for me to speak my truth, a private place where I could be honest.

I could write my story without anyone trying to interrupt me or put their spin on it. The only person I had to wrestle with were my own emotions. I had a rather difficult time at school, so I would write about the bad, tough days there. I was very shy, unconfident, rather homely, and was bullied a lot. Yup, I was!

I was the kid no one wanted for their team on sports days. Oh, how I hated those days. Two captains would be chosen, and they would go through the class and choose who they wanted on their team. I can still recall wanting desperately to disappear, to melt into the floor as name by name got called. All the other names, but never mine. It didn't matter who the captain was, or what day it was—I was always the last one picked.

Really, it's okay, don't feel sorry for me. I have done a lot of self-work to overcome being unconfident and co-dependent. I got rid of a lot of undesirable traits—because I wanted to. I did not want to be the person I had become. I somehow knew that there was more to life and more to me.

That is why I say to you, and will say it over and over again, that you always need to be working on yourself so that you can be the person you are meant to be. Never stop learning, never stop looking for answers, never be satisfied to come in last.

The work we do for ourselves should not end with this book. Let this book be just one part of the puzzle you are creating, the puzzle that will eventually reveal a new you.

As I am sitting here writing, I realize that I could go on and on about grief and recovery. There is just so much for me to tell you, so much for you to learn. I just may have to write Volume II.

I hope this book serves you well. I hope as you read the pages and stories you find your courage, your strength, and your purpose. But most importantly, I hope you now realize that even though your beloved is not with you any longer in the physical sense, they live on within your heart. And there they will stay forever. Guiding you, looking after you, loving you, and waiting patiently for you!

I wish you love, serenity, and enlightenment each day of your life.

CONCLUSION

Today Kenda Summers lives outside Chicago with her dog Stelly, a Goldendoodle who she has also trained to go on stage with her. Stelly the Golden Entrancer performs with Kenda in stage hypnosis and mentalism shows. She also accompanies Kenda to her clinical office to help relax clients who have high anxiety and stress.

She learns every day from the people who come into her life to share their story of loss with her. Witnessing others grief and just being a set of ears without judgement is one of the best gifts you can be to an individual who is grieving.

Its not easy to open your heart up to love again after you have suffered a loss. But grief as you know is the price we pay for love. Her wish is that you will allow your heart to overflow with love again when you are ready, just like she did with Stelly.

Please join my Pet Loss Facebook Group
at: www.facebook.com/groups/healingsolutionsforpetloss

For more information about my On-Line Grief School please
see: www.petsorrow.com

"Dogs come into our lives to teach us about love and loyalty. They depart to teach us about loss. A new dog never replaces an old dog; it merely expands the heart. If you have loved many dogs, your heart is very big." ~ Erica Jong

Printed in Great Britain
by Amazon

53769250R00104